Praise for
Bravery in Bits and Pieces

"After 80 years, Bonnie Byde's remarkable account of life in the Santo Tomas Internment camp during World War II is now in print! Conveying the stark realities of wartime, it describes a family's experience as mother, father, and two young children were interned by the Japanese army in the Philippines, confined for three years, and finally liberated. Especially highlighting the ways in which the war's horrors and privations affected the lives of the women and children, the story that unfolds in these pages also illustrates how one woman responded to the challenges with courage—and with eloquence. Readers will be grateful to Bonnie Byde's children, grandchildren, and great-grandchildren for sharing this unique account of wartime travails with a larger audience."

—Emily Rosenbery
Department of History
University of California, Irvine

66When I read *Bravery in Bits and Pieces* I was reminded of my own experiences as a small child during WWII. The experience of Ann's family was so much more. Her mother's beautifully written journal took me into the experience of being in an internment camp in the Philippines on a daily basis . . . on little pieces of paper. I found it spellbinding. It is a must read."

—*Judith Hunder*

66*Bravery: Courageous behavior or character*

To imagine the circumstances at Santo Tomas is beyond my comprehension.

To imagine the fear of misbehaving, even inadvertently, but at the cost of the lives of your children, is beyond my comprehension.

To know the courage and character it took to steal "Bits and Pieces" of paper and pencils in order to journal the events chronicled in this masterpiece will live in my memory forever."

—*Kathryn Habstritt*

For Carolyn,
From Bonn Byde Moeller

Bravery in Bits and Pieces:
Recollections of Santo Tomas

Bonnie Byde
preserved by Anita Moeller

This is a work of creative nonfiction. The events portrayed are to the best of Bonnie Byde's memory. While all the stories in this book are true, some names and identifying details have been changed to protect the privacy of the people involved.

Edited by Kerry Aberman

ISBN 13: 978-1-64343-649-4
Library of Congress Catalog Number: 2022915668

Printed in the United States of America
First Printing: 2022

26   25   24   23   22   5   4   3   2   1

Book design and typesetting by Tina Brackins.

This book is typeset in IvyJournal.

Cover photo: *Santo Tomas Internment Camp Liberation*, public domain, Wikimedia Commons.

Pond Reads Press
939 Seventh Street West
Saint Paul, MN 55102
(952) 829-8818
www.BeaversPondPress.com

Acknowledgements

Many thanks to my friends and family who encouraged me to keep this story alive for future generations. Thanks in particular to my daughter Elizabeth, who invited me to present this story to her elementary school class. Thanks to my son Eric, who passed the story on to his children. His son Gray, who turned it into a college thesis, and my son Mark who helped with the entire publishing process.

In addition, I'd like to thank my friends at Folkstone, especially those at our Friday night dinners, and the weekly Penguin cocktail parties. Many of you read my mother's memoir (which I had named *Recollections of Santo Tomas*). You came back to me bubbling over with enthusiasm and urging me to get it published. I had Mom's memoir in my possession for over forty-five years but had never considered publishing it. Your excitement made me take another look at the memoir.

Beaver's Pond Press in St. Paul, Minnesota also gave me positive encouragement. This book will be a gift for my children, their children, and Mom's relatives in Australia. This piece of history will introduce people who've never heard of the Philippine Islands to the horrors of World War II. It certainly showed me what a courageous mother I had.

The publisher, in consultation with the author's daughter, Anita Moeller, has opted to replace the word *Jap* wherever it appears with the word *Japanese.* The abbreviated word was in widespread use (including countless headlines of English-language newspapers) when Bonnie Byde used it. It has a different meaning to contemporary readers than it did to Bonnie or her original readers in 1944. In her own 1974 disclaimer she says, "Had I wished to downgrade them every time I spoke their name, I am sure I was mad enough at them at the time to have used stronger language." We do not believe Bonnie would want her priceless report to be associated with, or judged by, a highly offensive racial slur in 2023, the time of this publication. We agree with her that she could, and would, have used stronger language in 1944 if that was her intent. Thus, after much consideration and discussion, we've made the very serious decision to amend this source material.

Prologue

How did a midthirties businessman from Hawaii ever connect with a midtwenties secretary from Sydney, Australia? Read on.

Eric Byde was born in Husum, Germany in 1898. His parents, Ludwig and Luise Bydekarken, operated a small hotel in this North Sea town. The business struggled financially because of all the wars that plagued Germany. Eventually, they decided to sell the hotel and move to the United States having heard that land there was cheap.

They needed to reach the West Coast, but there was no Panama Canal in 1906. So, they made the trip the hard way, taking a ship from Germany to Panama, riding a train across the isthmus, then taking a northbound ship to California, where they settled in the San Jose area.

Eric was an only child. His parents enrolled him in school in Campbell, California. When he graduated from high school, he immediately joined the US Army. WWI was still raging. He also became a US citizen. Eric's parents were very upset that he was going to fight against "The Fatherland," so they decided to return to Germany when it was safe to do so. They did just that, leaving Eric all alone.

Eric became a "traveling man." He sailed from country to country, seeing the world. Whenever he became low on cash, he would play poker with the other passengers, winning enough to pay his way. When he reached Hawaii, he decided to stay there. He found a partner and started an automotive parts company.

Eric made a trip to Australia to drum up business. He stayed with a friend for a few days in New Zealand. His friend had a photograph of Jessie McLeod on his desk, and Eric commented on how pretty she was. His friend said she was only a good friend, and everyone who knew her called her *Bonnie*, the Scottish word for pretty.

"Hey Eric, you're going to Sydney, and Bonnie lives there too. I'm going to write you a letter of introduction so you can have a friend show you around."

Jessie McLeod was born in Melbourne, Australia in 1912. She was the third of four children. Her parents, Ruby and Arthur McLeod, operated a mom-and-pop grocery store. The business was on the first floor, and the family of six lived upstairs. There were some health issues in the family, so eventually they moved to Sydney where the weather was warmer.

Bonnie caught diphtheria in her teenage years. The only known treatment in those days was total quarantine. To achieve that, Bonnie was "shipped off" to an asylum in middle Australia where she had to stay all alone for a year to get well. Bonnie returned to school for her final years but became very unhappy. All the girls her age had graduated, and she was the new kid on the block.

Eric must have been a good salesman because he scored a date with Bonnie using an old trick. He had the letter of introduction but also brought a bouquet of flowers and a box of chocolates which he presented to Ruby! It was an instant hit!

Bonnie and Eric dated frequently for the next few weeks. On his last day in Australia, he proposed to Bonnie, but she said she needed more time to think about it. When Eric's ship arrived in Honolulu, he went immediately to the jewelry store and picked out a diamond engagement ring which he then mailed to Bonnie. That's all it took! She said yes and booked passage on the SS Lurline, arriving shortly after Christmas. They were married in January 1938. On February 26, 1939 their first child— that would be me, Ann Byde—was born. My brother, John, was born September 28, 1940.

Eric was still in the Philippines when John

was born. He and Bonnie discussed whether Eric should make the long, slow trip back to Hawaii to be there for John's birth. Bonnie had been gifted with all kinds of paid help, so she felt comfortable managing one more baby. When John was three months old, Bonnie packed up most of their belongings and bought tickets for The Philippine Clipper airplane. That flight took three nights and four days. Planes could not carry enough fuel to fly that far in one trip, so the company outfitted the three islands of Midway, Wake, and Guam into hotels. Passengers would stay overnight, shower, and eat breakfast before continuing onward.

Their plane was late arriving in Cavite, the harbor for Manila, because of an unexpected storm.

According to my mother, the first thing newcomers did was hire a cook, a driver, and an amah for each of their children. I was wondering what on earth a woman would do to keep busy, and she said they played cards, went bowling, (Nine Pines), and went out to dinner and parties a lot. My dad would often go to Mom's favorite dress shop and bring home a new dress for her to wear to the many parties they attended.

Once you read Bonnie's memoir, you'll understand what a shock the camp was to a person who had been pampered and waited on for three years.

—January 1974

It was not until during the Watergate Investigations in 1973 that the question arose as to whether the use of the term *Japs* rather than *Japanese* was degrading to the people of that nation.

I see where I have used the term throughout this letter, and I have tried to recollect how I was thinking at the time I wrote it. It is my honest opinion that in those days, the term was used as an abbreviation. Had I wished to degrade them every time I spoke their name, I am sure I was mad enough at them at the time to have used stronger language.

—*Bonnie Byde*

'Santo Tomas' Internment Camp,
MANILA, PHILIPPINE ISLANDS,
March 8th, 1944.

My Dear Mother and Dad:

So often during the past two years I have want-ed to put something down in writing about our life here so that you could read it later on; a diary would have been the best, but that has been almost impossible, owing—of course—to the constant fear of being searched. Some, I know, have taken that risk. There will doubtlessly be well-written day-by-day descriptions of this place, but having two children, I have felt (up until now) that it would not be fair of me to take any unnecessary chances. At this date, the risk does not appear to be very great, so I will try to go back to when the war started, to tell you what has taken place. And if things look bad later, I can always destroy this.

It is strange to look back now and remember how smug we were—thinking that trouble would not come to the Philippines and that if it did, the

Americans would take care of it right away. We quickly learned how wrong we were. Naturally, we were horrified to hear of the December 6, 1941 bombing of Pearl Harbor, and still more so by Baguio—it being so close—but still, the feeling that "it is not here" persisted. At three o'clock the next morning, the bombing of Nichol's Field had us out of bed quicker than a flash.

All I said at first was *bombs*. Eric tried to joke by saying "No, it's an earthquake." But we both knew, and the fear that gripped me was something quite different to anything I'd felt before. Luckily, the children continued to sleep, but we went outside where we were joined by our nearest neighbors—Doris and Gene Mueller, and Doctor and Mrs. Kui. For a while, the tracer bullets could be seen. Then all was quiet once more and we discussed the possibilities of making our places safer. We were able to use our basements for fairly good protection against shrapnel, so daylight found us all busy cleaning our individual places and making them as secure as possible. After the initial fear, there was a feeling of utter helplessness about how to protect the children from this. Later, when the bombings became a daily occurrence, we mostly felt a terrible anger against the Japanese. But there was nothing we could do about it.

We agreed the most important thing was not to alarm the children (if it could be helped), so at night when the siren sounded, Eric and I dressed quickly and just sat in the dark waiting. Necessary things had already been packed in hand cases and placed ready by the door along with blankets for the children. Luckily, we never had to disturb their sleep. The daytime was different though; when the siren sounded we would go downstairs to the basement and wait in one particular corner that seemed the best protected.

We would make the children as comfortable as possible, using a grass mat and some of the loose cushions from upstairs. I often think of the many tins of cookies I allowed the kids to consume during those hours, just to keep them quiet. With Ann and John, we had to pretend the whole thing was fun—not so much with John perhaps, as he was too young to understand—but Ann was forever asking questions. We always told her they were playing games and that this was just part of it, and I told the servants they were never to show any signs of fear in front of the children.

After the bombing of Cavite, Louise and Martin Craven closed their apartment and came to stay with us; it seemed too dangerous for them near the waterfront. Then later, Vee and Bill Jones and their children, Patricia and Jacqueline, came to stay; their home in Pasay had been bombed, and they'd lost everything. I was so glad our house was large. I began to count just how many we could take if things continued this way. On account of the raids, we could not be sure of the usual deliveries from the cold stores and grocers, so I bought a supply of things including yeast and began making bread each day. This kept me busy, as I now had to prepare food for ten people. It was too much for the cook to handle; besides, I wanted to be sure there was no waste because I didn't know what was going to happen next. The Japanese almost always chose the noon hour for their raids, so the children's lunches had to be carried downstairs. It seemed as though everything I started to do would be interrupted by raids, so after a while, I would watch. The planes always came from the same direction and passed (often over our house) on toward Manila. If I could see that they would not pass directly overhead, I would stay upstairs and go on with my work. The servants were very good during those weeks, but they were terribly scared. Many people lost their servants right at the beginning when, in panic, their hired help fled back to their own provinces.

One bad day that sticks in my memory was the day they bombed Camp Murphy and Zablan Field. These places were close to our house but had been passed over day in, day out without so much as being fired at. But this time, when Eric and Martin were downtown and I was busy in the kitchen, I heard the usual drone of the planes. I sent the others downstairs while I watched through the living room windows. I could tell they would pass a little to one side, so I decided to stay upstairs and watch this long row of planes come nearer and nearer.

I wished—as I had wished every time—that they would hurry and sound the siren. For some reason, this was always slow. In most cases, the planes passed our house and were well on their way to their target before the siren sounded. When they were out of sight overhead, I ran across the house and looked out the porch windows just in time to see and hear those dreadful explosions. They shook the house badly, so I rushed downstairs to be with the children. Very soon, there was plenty of action. Our planes had gone up to intercept the Japanese and quite a dogfight ensued. The noise seemed deafening, and while I realize that compared to fights taking place in other parts of the world, this must have been very small, it was our first one and so, to us, seemed bad.

During the fight I peeped out to see what was happening. There were Filipino soldiers in the long grasses near our house. One gesticulated wildly at me to remove a long line of laundry we had out. I dashed out and have never moved so quickly before. I let the clothes pins fly anywhere and in the middle of it, I looked up to see a row of Japanese planes almost overhead. I admit I felt scared. After the raid was over, we heard that a bullet had gone right through our neighbor's roof and ceiling, landing on their table. Later, when Eric and Martin came home, we learned that they had spent a hectic time on their stomachs in a ditch during the fight. Christmas Day finally came and I was thankful I had shopped before the war started. I was determined for the kids to have some fun, so we tied all their presents in red paper and put them into pillowcases. They thought it was all quite wonderful, and being so young, they didn't miss a Christmas tree. We managed to prepare quite a festive meal consisting of duck and most of the trimmings. Soon after the bombings had started, we'd sent the cook and the houseboy to a market to buy live chickens and ducks. We'd had the idea to keep them and fatten them up for possible use in the future. They'd been a weary bunch of birds and had started to fall rapidly, so commencing with the ducks, we'd begun to kill and eat them before they died. Our Christmas dinner, like all other noon meals, was interrupted by a raid. We parked everything in the oven and spent an hour or so in the basement while the menfolk cussed out the Japanese and all their ancestors.

There are other incidents that took place during those weeks of bombings, but they seem of little interest now, so I won't waste time writing them down. Everything seemed to happen so quickly during those days. We learned Manila would not be treated as an open city, and that the Japanese were expected to enter it in just a day or so. We frantically rushed to buy canned goods, but it was a hard job because we didn't have much money on hand and Alfonso SyCip, the head of Yek Nua Trading and Co., had fled the city along with other Chinese leaders, leaving us an unsigned cheque. The banks closed the next day, so we were out of luck. From our house looking towards Manila, it seemed as though the whole town was ablaze. Black smoke rolled upwards from many points. It was quite a sight. Oil and gasoline had been poured into the river and set afire. I don't know what gave us this impression, but as a group we thought that after the Japanese took over the city and registered us, we would be permitted to go on living (more or less) as before. Eric and Martin later admitted that they expected to be taken and put to work, but they did not say so at the time for fear of alarming us. No one expected the women and children to be treated as they were. In fact, looking back, it is not really the short war that I remember, so much as the incident I am about to relay, and our lives from this point on.

During the first Sunday—two days, I think, after occupation—our friend Ann Bachrach telephoned to say we had better be prepared and to pack enough things for three days. She had heard they were picking up enemy nationals—us—and taking them to a central place. She told us not to be afraid because they were very kind and were not out to harm us. She is a Filipino citizen and went on to say that an officer and his men had called to "borrow" her car, but that they were extremely polite. This eased our minds because up to then, we felt dreadful not knowing what was going to happen or how. We wondered if they might kill us outright, or worse—if they should harm the children while we were powerless to stop them. We sat around all day, playing bridge between meals to pass the time. We all felt very nervous. About nine o'clock that night, this same friend telephoned again to say not to retire too early as they were still on the job and had just picked up some people in her district. At about eleven thirty, we decided that we had better go to bed. (I forgot to say that the morning the Japanese entered the city, Vee and Bull Jones decided they would feel safer with a larger group of people, so they moved downtown to the Manila Club.) No sooner had we undressed when we heard a commotion at the front gates. We redressed in great haste. We have often said since, *if we had only known who they were and had kept the lights off and stayed quiet, the incident may never have occurred.* But we thought we were doing the right thing to let them in.

There were two Japanese, one in civilian attire and the other in a soldier's uniform. The latter had two revolvers which made him look like a holdup man in a film. Both were obviously under the influence of liquor because they had difficulty reaching the top step. They waved about in a sickly manner. It did not occur to me that this was not an official visit; I did not yet know their methods for dealing with us. The civilian spoke all the time as the other could not manage English at all. He made a pretense of being official and said he represented the Japanese Government and that we were to do as he said. We were told to raise our hands above our heads. We probably looked foolish but were too scared to think of it. He then asked for our passports, which I had to explain were in the other room. He didn't seem to understand too well and did a lot of grunting (a peculiar habit of the Japanese), but finally he seemed to agree that I could go and get them. I don't think he trusted Eric. I turned my back and went to the bedroom, but I didn't feel too good knowing those revolvers were pointing at my back. I was quick, you can be sure. He looked to be examining our passports, though I feel sure he didn't understand a thing in them. He then demanded gasoline. We didn't have any more than what was in the tank of the car, and we said so.

He asked three times, then said, "three times I ask gasoline—if tomorrow come, find gasoline, we shoot." He then asked for guns or ammunition and wound up his demand with the same threat. I think it was at this time that the fellow with the guns decided we weren't taking him seriously enough, because he took a quick step forward and fired one gun within a couple inches of Eric and Martin's chests. He fired crosswise and the bullet went through the wall of Ann's bedroom. My heart and everything inside me seemed to concentrate in the pit of my stomach, and I remember thinking, *well, I suppose this is the finish*. I fully expected more gunfire to follow. Eric turned about three shades of gray. Johnny woke up and began to cry violently. Then the civilian motioned for us to go inside to the dining room, and when there, he asked us for whiskey, which I was thankful to say we didn't have. I'd had the bright idea during the day to pour all the liquid refreshment down the sink. He then asked for flashlights, batteries, and cameras—Martin had to part with a beauty—and finally, our jewelry and money. This little tableau was beginning to look ridiculous, but faced with loaded revolvers, we didn't quibble. I stupidly had on my diamond wristwatch, which I valued more than anything. It was my first Christmas present from Eric, and after a glance at Eric, who nodded *yes*, I took it off and put it on the growing pile on the table. At this stage, Johnny was really carrying on with his crying, so I asked their permission to pick him up, which they granted.

I carried him on my left arm, and upon rejoining the group, the soldier made facial expressions that implied he liked babies. He came and stood close to me. It was evident he wanted to pat the child, but didn't dare put his gun down, so with the back of his right hand (which was in a nasty black glove), he began to stroke Johnny down the right side of his face, making weird noises. This brought the firing end of the gun within an inch of my face, and considering the inebriated state of the fellow, I found myself watching his trigger finger in a sort of stupid fascination. Johnny howled his protest, so finally, the Japanese quit and stepped back near his companion who then ordered Louise to put all the jewelry and goods into the soldier's pocket. After that, the civilian reiterated that he had asked three times for gasoline, guns, jewelry, etc. and that if any of these things were found when they came the next day, we would all be shot. He then said we would be taken the next day to Santo Tomas Internment Camp, where we'd be held for about three days, so to be packed and ready. He took the keys to the car and front door, and threatened that if we left the house, tried to follow them, or contacted anyone, we would be shot. They weaved their way out. When we heard the car drive off, we just looked stupidly at each other. Then my knees gave way and I had to sit down quickly. It was a hard job not to cry, though the tears were mostly in anger at the injustice of being treated in such a manner, and of the dreadful uncertainty of the past hour.

The servants came upstairs with wide eyes. They didn't know what to make of it at all. In a little while, we heard a shot come from the next house which was empty because the occupants had all gone downtown. Later, there was another shot from Byron Ford's house. We hoped they were all OK. Gene and Doris Mueller hadn't been bothered after they explained that they were Swiss because the fellows were only after Americans. We spent the rest of the night packing and repacking our bags, and worrying as to what we would need; we also realized we could all be separated, and though Eric got stubborn at this stage and didn't want to take any food for himself, I put as many cans as I could among his clothes. I had the two children, and I didn't know how I was going to manage them, plus cases *and* food enough for the three of us. Johnny, though fifteen months old, was still on a bottle because he had such trouble with his teeth. He was rejecting food so much that we were only sure of him getting enough nourishment if we kept him on the bottle. He was taking a special soya-malt powdered milk at the time, so I had to pack a few cans of that. Poor Mening—Johnny's Amah—fell to the floor, and with tears rolling down her cheeks and her arms wrapped around my knees in a very dramatic fashion, she wailed, "Oh Mum, what will happen to the children?"

I certainly didn't know, but I said, "get up and don't be a foolish girl; everything will be alright." I sent her to get things for me to pack. When it was done, we sat around. Towards morning, Consuelo Ford telephoned. After enquiring about each other's welfare—they had faired the same as us except their houseboy had been badly beaten up, and because Byron had liquor in his house, he'd had to sit down and drink with those dreadful fellows—Consuelo said she was convinced the visit was unofficial and that the fellows were just looters.

She asked if I would stand by her if she reported it. I said I would, so she got in touch with Japanese officials downtown who apparently were very polite, listened to her story, and said that it should not have happened and that if they caught the culprits, our things would be returned. During the morning, a member of the Manila Police came to take a report. When I came to my watch, he smiled and said, "I'll turn this report in, but I don't think you'll ever see your things again. They like watches especially." Pointing to a paler mark on his own wrist, he said, "you see, they just demand them from anyone." Perhaps I seem to have gone into too much detail about this one small episode, but remember, this was our first dealing with the enemy, and it left an impression. No one called to pick us up that day, and by late afternoon we received a message from the Fathers of the Catholic Seminary a few blocks away. They said those looters had been around the entire neighborhood, and that if we felt afraid of further visits, we could come stay at the Seminary. At first, we didn't think of doing this. But as darkness came, we thought how foolish we were to take risks with the children. You see, even if the Japanese were in the wrong, we were not able to take any steps to defend ourselves because as soon as Manila was occupied, a proclamation came in large print in a special paper. It said if any Japanese was assaulted, killed, or harmed in any way, the culprit would be shot at once, and if the culprit could not be found, then fifteen people from that district would be shot instead. With this in mind, we rolled up our mattresses and with our bags, went to the Seminary. On arriving there, we found the place crowded with people of all nationalities. The Fathers, or Brothers—I'm not sure of these people's titles—had very kindly vacated their rooms and centralized themselves in a smaller space so that each family was permitted a small room. This place showed me the extent to which these people go without everyday comforts while pursuing their religion. Their rooms were nothing more than a small cubicle containing one narrow bed without springs, one small wooden table, and one uncomfortable wooden chair. There were no trimmings whatsoever, and the rest of the building was along the same order—cold and cheerless. No doubt, they get used to it. We put one mattress on the bed, and for convenience, Eric slept there while I put the other two mattresses together on the floor and slept with a child on either side. We spent Monday night, Tuesday, and Wednesday there. As it was our first taste of discomfort, it seemed quite a nightmare. The servants had come along with us as they were afraid to stay alone, and they all slept on the floor outside the room. During the day, we would send them back to the house to prepare food, and this we ate just standing about or sitting on the Seminary's floor.

The most dreadful part of our short stay in this

place was having to use the toilets—pardon my mentioning this subject, but during these long months, we had seen so many dreadful things that to speak of them doesn't really bother me anymore and you may as well hear all the nasty details. Without becoming really crude, words cannot describe these facilities; naturally, the Fathers were living quietly alone in their section, and there wasn't anyone in charge of the rest of us. Wherever there is a crowd, it is essential to have some order, but since there was none, no one did any cleaning of this public place. While you can see people washing their clothes day in and out, the majority of them seem to have no idea of how to keep a toilet clean, or even how to use one in a civilized manner. Well, I'll skip further details of this.

On Thursday morning, Japanese officials arrived and gathered all of us who were staying at the Seminary. They said they would give us two hours to be ready to leave. These two hours turned out to be little more than half an hour, so we didn't even have time to eat lunch as we hoped we would. We crammed our things back into our bags and assembled out in front of the building. The following two hours is a time I shall always remember, and though we are taught to "love our enemies," if I live to be a hundred, I will not.

Johnny had a terrific fever of 104 degrees that day, and I was naturally quite worried about him. Well, the head Father very kindly spoke to the

Japanese in charge and really pleaded with him to allow me to stay there with the children at least until the little one was better. He said he would be responsible, but the fellow just wouldn't listen to him, and grunted that the women and children must go along too. When we discussed it later, it seemed to us that the Japanese must have thought we had come to this place in the hopes of evading internment, because compared to the stories most people tell of being picked up, they were especially mean to us. Though of course, in comparison, we haven't spoken to many.

There was one instance where some Japanese had collected the Americans and others from an entire court of houses and made them all sit on the ground in the blazing sun for a couple of hours while several Japanese soldiers sat nearby busily sharpening their long swords. You can imagine how these poor folk felt, expecting, of course, to lose their heads at any time and wondering how long they had, whereas what actually happened was that a truck drove up, piled them all in, and took them to the camp. But I feel sure the waiting must have scared at least six months of life out of them.

To get back to us . . . this Thursday was a cloudless day. The noon sun was extremely hot, and but for a few trees close to the fence, the front lawn was bare and scorched. They had us line up on either side of a path—Filipinos on one side and other nationalities on the other. Then the Japanese in charge, speaking through an interpreter, demanded any guns, knives, cameras, flashlights, etc. After wasting endless time over these requests, they finally started to sort us out into groups. Being the only Australian (though my children are American), I found myself isolated with Johnny in my arms and Ann clinging very scared to my dress. Johnny, by this time, was becoming terribly heavy, and I must have looked about as pale as I felt because a British fellow who apparently was a little less scared than the rest, ignored the demand to stand still and calmly went and found me a chair. He put it under a tree for me. The Japanese looked on but didn't protest, so that was a help. After that, they placed a table with a fellow at it and we had to file past showing our passports and giving such details of ourselves as he demanded before returning to our places. All this, as I said, took the best part of two hours, and at the end of this time, the Americans, British, and so forth were motioned to two buses. Filipinos, Filipino citizens, and other neutrals were told to remain, while the rest of us were packed into the buses. I was going to say "like sardines," but sardines are packed properly—with us, the soldier just stood at the door and kept ordering us in even though the bus was full. By the time we were in with our bags and mattresses, we were all over each other. I had quite a time finding a hole through the cases above me for the children to breathe through; I had been among the first to get in, while Eric had to wait out with a few of the men to load the baggage. He was nowhere near to help me. They drove us to Santo Tomas University, which, as you enter, looks pleasant enough, being a huge building set in quite spacious grounds. As we drove up the drive and saw all the other white people—many of whom were friends—I almost sighed with relief to be among them after the previous few days. We alighted and had to line up, open our bags for inspection, then stand behind them till the job was over.

One rather kindly Japanese, on seeing me trying to comfort Johnny, said to me, "Baby sick?" and I said *yes, very sick.* He said, "You get pass, take baby home, me show." He directed me to go to the Japanese office and ask for a release, but this was as far as he would help me, so I left the group, and went to wait in the office for a terrible time before being able to speak to an official. It seemed that a great number of people had the same idea about being released. Some, who I suppose were better talkers than others, managed it. But when it came to my turn, I was out of luck because the Japanese looked as though he'd heard quite enough of it. He told me it had just been decided that in all cases of sickness, we had to go through our own doctors, so I was directed across the campus to what had been fixed up quickly as a hospital, and there I waited my turn again before finally seeing

Dr. Leach. Perhaps he was working under a threat not to be too lenient—I wouldn't know. However, he said, "Well, after all, fevers in small children don't usually mean much, and the child is sure to be alright," and with that, he wrote me out a chit which permitted me to use a stove in the back of what had been the campus restaurant in order to fix John's milk. And that was that.

Then, as it was getting late, I started the frantic search for a space. Here is where things really began to break one's heart in earnest. You see, the University is just a large, square, very-plain concrete building comprised of about one hundred bare schoolrooms. Within these, we had to find spaces on the floor for our mattresses, or, if you didn't have one, just reserve an area of concrete. The Japanese insisted that the sexes be separated, so some rooms were for men, and others for women and children. At this date, January 8th, 1942, there was no order such as we have today, so those who arrived first—from January 3rd on, I think—naturally took the best places such as near the windows or doors, or at least around the walls. Even though we saw room to spare on the first and second floors, people were surprisingly selfish, and in each case, we were told "no more room in here," and were turned away. We finally wound up on the third floor and managed to squeeze in. I had one three-quarter size mattress and one crib mattress for the three of us, and we were luckier than some.

Eric hadn't brought one for himself because with the suitcases, we had all we could manage. Then, too, the men still expected to be sent somewhere else and didn't think they would be permitted such a luxury, so Eric found himself a piece of concrete on the ground floor, while Martin picked the third floor. The poor fellow was very upset at having to leave Louise with all those people and naturally he worried as to how they would treat her, but there was nothing he could do about it.

After parking our things, I left Eric to mind the children on the front lawn while I went to make up a bottle for John. Everyone working in the kitchen seemed to think they had a right to bar anyone else admission, and I had to flourish my chit under their noses and stick to my guns. Finally, I finished and almost wished it wasn't the tropics so that I could have made more than one at a time. I fed Johnny while Eric opened some cold, canned food for Ann. It was then dusk, time to return to the building, so up we trudged, carrying the children to the third floor. When I put them on the mattresses, the hopelessness of it all: how to continue to live in this dreadful fashion, keep the children clean and fed, and confine them to this space on the floor, seemed too much for me to figure out. I was hungry too, as I hadn't eaten since breakfast and had carried Johnny almost the whole day. I remember I just dissolved into tears regardless of the other occupants in the room. That had been the only real cry I've had in all this time because even though I have often felt like crying—and no doubt, a good cry would have helped sometimes—one really needs some privacy for that sort of thing, and in this place, privacy is one of the things we have absolutely none of. That first night was a terrible nightmare. I put the children on the wall side, one on either end of the bigger mattress, while I reclined on the baby mattress to keep an eye on them. Of course, I didn't sleep a wink because Johnny was really sick and the Japanese kept wandering along the corridors peeping in at us. Traffic between the floors at night was prohibited, so help from Eric was out of the question. When Johnny developed convulsions, I took him to the nearest guard who gave me permission to take him to the ground floor first aid station. There, they gave him paregoric and later on, he slept a little and seemed a little less restless.

The first week of life in the camp is quite hazy to me now, as I seemed to be living in a kind of daze. I know I didn't eat for three days, and I think Eric only had some coffee which he had to wait in a long line for. Each bottle time for Johnny was a headache, and in one instance some woman said she was in charge of the kitchen and that I would have to leave as she couldn't have "just everyone" using the stoves when they were busy.

At this, I got tough and said, "my baby has to be fed, so you just try and throw me out." About the third day, Louise (whom I left in charge of the house, food, and whatever else there was) apparently got organized and heard they were permitting food into the Internees, because Primo (the cook) arrived at the fence with a package of food for us. This, we consumed with great enthusiasm right there on the lawn, and for a while, packages came in about every other day.

So many things should be said of these first days, yet how to put them and in what order is quite a problem. The Japanese commandant of the camp had chosen a few of our men to act as go-betweens for the Japanese to issue orders through. The power to organize things and to do a great deal for the comfort of the internees was apparently in their hands. The magnitude of their job was really terrific, and while they accomplished much, there is no doubt now that much more could have been done in those days when the Japanese were comparatively lenient. However, where we made the greatest mistake—and I think I'm right in saying that almost everyone made it—was to believe the stupid propaganda going out over the radio from the "Voice of Freedom." It was brought to us through our servants and friends on the outside, and it told us that "Help was on the way." Even today, the phrase *Help is on the way* is a standing joke in camp. This was especially true where the women and children were concerned because we really believed it would only be a short time before the

Japanese made some provision for us—the women and children—to return to our homes. This was never forthcoming, but plenty of people were granted releases for one reason or another; women with children one year and under were allowed to stay out, so I was out of luck there as Johnny was sixteen months. Many people I heard about did some heavy bribing, while others just did some good talking. Naturally, Eric was irate at being in a position of such helplessness. On the one hand, he wished he could get me out of there, while on the other, he realized that there at least he knew I was alright and could be of some help with the children. Outside, I would have needed money to live, and the only people I could have expected help from in that regard was Eric's agent, Alfonso SyCip, and here we were again out of luck. The Japanese collected old Alfonso quite early and charged him with aiding the Japanese boycott. They sentenced him to twenty years in prison. The rest of his family were turned out of their home and hounded for months. They were forced, as were all other wealthy Chinese, to give large sums of money to the Japanese. These, ironically enough, were spoken of in the local paper as "donations generously contributed by the Chinese community." We are, more or less, used to living in this mass manner now, but the memory of the first weeks will always remain: Japanese soldiers stomping along the corridors and peering into the rooms at any hour of the night just to look at us sleeping—or trying to sleep—on the floor; the first foodless days and the pride that kept us from asking for a meal ticket to permit us to obtain a meal from the camp kitchen; the first shower in full view of dozens of women; the endless lines— to wait in each time you had to use a toilet, to have a wash, to get a cup of coffee, to use a faucet or wash your clothes, to have a doctor see your child, and later, the dreadful lines to wait for food, with Ann whimpering by my side and Johnny in my arms; the times I climbed those concrete stairs with a child in each arm; the wakeful nights with children crying—first one then another; the children's objection (especially the little ones), to the cold showers—it was all they could have, so it was fortunate we were in the tropics where it wasn't too bad—they got fairly used to it; of the horrible feeling of having to wear rough dry clothes; and countless other things, but these seem to stick in my memory most.

About the second week, it was decided that all mothers and their children would be housed in a small frame building called the *Annex*, which was at the rear of the main building. This transfer was made, and it was such a relief to be spared all that stair climbing. This building is an oblong shape with rooms evenly spaced on either side of an uncovered walk. One room was set aside as a dining room and had rows of wooden benches on either side of wooden tables. The next room was turned into a kitchen where cooking was carried out for this group alone. Then, there were about fifteen other rooms where we all slept on the floor. Each morning we rolled up our mattresses, washed and cleaned our space, and put the mattresses down again because they were all we had to sit on to attend to the children or anything else.

In each room, one woman was elected "monitor" and any new rules were given to us through her. It was also her job to see that everyone kept their spaces clean and tidy, and to make a schedule under which we each took a turn at cleaning the toilet and shower room. It was our duty to wipe off the toilets after each use with a cloth dipped in disinfectant solution, to keep the floor mopped, and to see that children did not hold up the line unnecessarily. This duty usually came in half-hour stretches every other day so that all women took their turn. In the main building, the same duty was done in one hour stretches, but as there were so many more women per bathroom, your turn only came about every three weeks.

All able-bodied men were expected to get a job on some detail, so Eric took one on the serving line at the central kitchen which had been newly formed. The restaurant kitchen was done away with after the first few weeks except for special diet cases. Here, he poured tea in the afternoons and coffee in the mornings for two-hour stretches. Later, he transferred to the kitchen itself, and became a mush cook, which meant he had to get up at 4 a.m. each day to help cook the breakfast cereal; now, since the new "early roll call" he has to be up at 3 a.m.

In January, a lone plane flew over one night and dropped some bombs nearby. The Japanese anti-aircraft guns got into action and the poor Annex trembled. In the absence of air raid shelters, no one knew quite how to act, and some women woke their children and ran wildly about. I contemplated rolling mine off the mattress and using it as a cover, but after a while, the noise subsided and things seemed alright, so I didn't wake them. Everyone was quite excited and thought help had really come, but, of course, it was only one plane; if we had known then just how far away help really was, and how long we were doomed to stay in this place, I think many would have cracked up right then. It has been the constant thought of "only a few more months" that has kept most of us going.

During the last few days of January, John started to run fevers again and would not eat a thing; he also developed terrible diarrhea. I saw Dr. Whittaker, who pressed me to let him send John to the Philippine General Hospital before he became really ill; there, he would be cared for properly. I should have acted according to my instincts, which told me he was only teething, but being worried about the improper food and housing here, I said alright. Permission was granted through the Japanese in the central office in a very short time, and before I could think again, someone came and said "Have the baby ready right away as the bus for the hospital is about to leave." I suppose it was because I had a second child that the pass did not include me, so I had to hand Johnny—with his very high fever—to some woman who was also sick, to hold and to hand over to the hospital on arrival. This broke me up considerably as it seemed a most unnatural procedure to part a mother from her sick child. The next day, after haggling in the office for a long time, I received a pass to go on the bus to visit Johnny for one hour. Eric took care of Ann. At the hospital, I had lots of trouble because they said he wasn't there, and it turned out that the woman who carried him had to admit him under her own name because of the absence of the child's mother. I finally located the little fellow who was crying bitterly and clung to me the whole time. I was torn between taking him right back with me, or doing what I supposed was the right thing for him. Finally—and I will never forgive myself for it—I tore myself away.

The next day I took ill and was put in the camp hospital with the flu and an attack of nerves. Ann was a dear throughout all this and behaved wonderfully for the other women in the room who took care of her at night, while Eric and 'Uncle Martin' looked after her during the day. After a week of this, I snapped out of it and started hounding the office for permission to see John again, but all I got was the use of the telephone on a couple of occasions, over which I was told he was "doing alright."

During this time, a portion of the Holy Ghost Catholic Convent had been turned over to Dr. Del Mundo—a Filipina—to be used by children whose parents felt they would be better off there, away from the crowds. They had Filipino help, proper beds, better food, and the children were supposed to get the best of attention, but unless the child was under one year, the mother had to stay in camp. Dr. Whittaker urged me to let them send John there when he was well enough, and though I was against it for having to be parted from him, I finally thought it would be better for him. After six weeks in the downtown hospital, he was transferred to the children's home, and when the next visiting day came (once every two weeks) the bus brought all the children in to camp for one hour. We were appalled at the change in John; he had lost so much weight and was so quiet and pale. The memory of the crying that went on both with parents and children when the hour was up is one that still gives me chills, and I hate to even recall it. Even men looking on seemed so upset they had to turn away. During the next few weeks, they changed plans and allowed the parents to go in the bus to visit the children. Poor Johnny was nearly always in the sickroom with a fever. When I asked the doctor for information on him, she used to reply that he was alright and just weak from his long sickness. All this time, I was pestering the office for permission to take Ann and stay at the Holy Ghost, because, after all, there were many things in its favour—no lines to wait in, the proper-sized chairs and tables for the children, far less noise and confusion, proper beds to sleep in, and above all, a warm bath for them each day. Finally, they gave in and raised the age limit, but there are a few things I have left out that happened during February and March, and perhaps a little more detail about camp life would be in order at this time.

We had heard from Louise Craven that she and Mrs. Roy Bennett (who used to live near us), had gone to live together at another address in Quezon City, and that our servants had gone home to their provinces. Later, Martin was taken to St. Luke's Hospital to have his appendix removed, so Louise left our old district and went to live downtown to be near him. Visiting was allowed at the hospitals outside, so they were able to be together part of the time. Naturally, this meant an end to the odd packages of food that Louise used to send us, and at the same time, we heard the owner of the house we used to live in had re-rented it to some Swiss people. Martin could not be of any assistance, financial or otherwise, to Louise while she lived outside, so he obtained permission for her to be an internee, and when he came back from the hospital, she came in with him. She was able to bring a few extra pieces of clothing for us, but didn't have room for much.

For a week in February, I had a bad case of tonsilitis, but Eric and Ann kept well. Despite the fact that a lot of people seemed to think we should just sit and wait for help, the committee went ahead and did quite a lot to aid life here. Laundry troughs were installed—long, narrow tin arrangements about eighteen inches by twenty-four feet. The faucets were placed rather close together, so to do our laundry we stand at a space which will barely take a normal dishpan. The one I had sent in from the house is oval, and about twenty-four inches by sixteen inches; it just squeezes in, so doing sheets and blankets under these conditions is rather difficult. Drying lines were hung, and later, a dishwashing unit was set up. At all these facilities, it is usual to wait in a long line.

It was early in February when a tragedy befell the camp; three internees went over the wall. They were captured, and while we understand that in the rules such an offense merits a thirty-day stretch in jail, these men were terribly beaten up, then taken downtown—apparently to Santiago. We thought they had received enough punishment and were shocked to learn that they were shot. One fellow, "Blakey" Laycock, was an Australian. I had met him at Joan Hunter's house before the war and again during the Japanese bombing. The gloom that hung over the camp at this act was terrible, and some of our men really looked murderous; I hope they get their revenge someday. Perhaps I should mention the room I lived in—No. 71 in the Annex was, of course, a schoolroom and was reasonably large, but then it was filled to proportion. I think it first housed twenty-nine people, and when you consider this many people sleeping on the floor, it was quite a crush; in fact, it was just possible for a person to get between the beds if she walked sideways. At first, we were not allowed so much as a shelf, so everything had to be tucked back in our cases. Later, I was able to nail a small box to the wall at my space to use for cups, plates, etc., and later still, if one could wangle enough space, sets of shelves—and in some instances small cupboards—were permitted, but that was after they commenced to issue camp-made wooden beds. Then all our cases, etc., had to be parked under our beds. In the main building, the people were packed even closer together, and in many rooms there were lots of double-decker iron beds (old army beds, I believe), so the only saving grace was, and still is, that the ceilings are very high. Even so, this business of being close enough to hear your neighbor breathe will never cease to be repulsive. I'm afraid it will be quite a job to get the children to sleep in a room alone after this, as they are not only used to having their mothers either with them or right beside them, but there are dozens of other people, and especially children, to keep them company.

On April 2, Ann and I left Eric and went to the convent to be with Johnny. When I really moved in and could see him every day, I saw what a pitiful condition he was in. He was thin and pale with large dark eyes that seemed to just stare; he had some awful sores on the back of his head that spread from his hairline to his crown and almost across to each ear. He also had one big one on his foot. The doctor was giving him liver shots, but they weren't helping. He hadn't any appetite, and was left in his bed all day. Upon investigating, I found that while at the Philippine General Hospital, even though I had explained thoroughly the reason for his being on a bottle, and had given them proper instructions on how to fix his milk, they had deliberately ignored it, and had never given him any. The cans of his special soya malt milk were all intact—never having been opened. No wonder he went down rapidly, and remembering the trouble I had with John until we found this particular milk that agreed with him, it made me wonder just what he had eaten while there. Since all this had been done, there was no point in putting him back on a bottle, but I did instruct them to give him a glass of soya milk each day at the convent. He had little interest in it the few times I saw him at meals.

The setup there was rather nerve-racking insofar as the mothers were housed in a building apart and were only allowed to go to the children's rooms at certain hours. At meal times, mothers were strictly taboo. While this may have worked in some cases, it upset me because I knew I could get John to eat better than any other girl. Another thing I didn't like was that because the staff were all ardent Catholics, from around six to seven each morning, they were all at mass, and I discovered that even the sick kiddies were left entirely alone during this hour. Many, like John, were small and quite able to climb out of their cots. This worried me to no end, and a few times I just ignored the rules and went to their building. Often, I found John had been lying in a wet diaper and was sore, uncomfortable, and crying. On one occasion, when the Mother Superior from the convent was making her rounds of the place, she saw me with Johnny and said "Oh, are you this little child's mother?" When I assured her I was, she said she had been watching him because he looked so ill, and she hoped he was baptized. I said he wasn't, and she became quite worried and pressed me to let her make arrangements to have it done right away because, she said, by the look of the child, she felt sure "God was calling him, and would probably take him away." This really burned me up—she looked so cool and sanctimonious and sure of herself—so I said rather heatedly that I wasn't a Catholic, and that no one was going to take the child away; he was going to get better, and I would see to it myself that he did, so baptizing a sick child didn't interest me at all. The poor soul was much distressed at my outburst and looked really shocked.

I could see they needed more help at this place and that the children were not getting anywhere near the attention they should. Well, I put up with it for just one week and then asked Dr. Del Mundo for permission to let me take John to St. Luke's Hospital for a thorough check up; this, she gave me. So, without notifying the office at Santo Tomas, I packed up, called a *caratela*, and set off. The doctor wanted me to leave Ann there but I said, "No, I'll stick to both children and then I know what's going on." This was my first ride in a caratela, which is a cart on two wheels, drawn by a very frail-looking pony—usually all bones and hungry looking—and I was scared stiff. Every step the horse took, I thought he would fall down. But he didn't, and we finally reached the hospital. I remember Stan Kingsbury was on the front porch at the time and came down to greet me, but when he started to remark how bad John looked, I just couldn't talk to him. I was so upset and nervous, and so near tears.

Well, we settled down with a certain feeling of relief to be in capable hands. I told them to check John thoroughly and for Dr. Fletcher to examine him on his next visit from the camp. The first thing they did was to shave John's head, and the poor kid fussed so that we had to wrap him entirely in a sheet to hold him in place. Well, he was checked over again and again by Dr. Fletcher who happened to come the next day. He said they were cross at the office because I had made the move without their permission, but I didn't care and said so. Luckily, I never heard any more about it. The finding on Johnny was malnutrition, acute anemia, and chronic bronchitis, plus the awful sores. They commenced the proper treatment and diet for him, and each day he had ultraviolet light treatments for his head and foot. By the way, while at the convent, Ann had caught her finger in a *bahooka* (split bamboo) mattress, and it had become infected and had to be treated each day. It was very painful, but apart from that, she was well and without trouble. We stayed at St. Luke's for six and a half weeks, and during this time John got slowly-but-surely better, but Ann's finger got worse despite the constant treatment. Finally, they had to freeze her finger top and remove the nail. After that, it healed and later the new nail appeared. Ann also developed a bad sore throat, and the doctor said as her tonsils were quite large. He suggested it would be wise to remove them when the infection was better.

Eric had received permission to come to see us once, and I told him that I had been able to contact John SyCip who'd given me some money and offered a home for myself and the children if I could get permission to live outside the camp, as many were doing at that date. We talked it over and decided that since the Japanese kept check on that family, it might not be too safe. I had experienced all I wanted of the convent, so the only thing left was to return to Santo Tomas when my pass expired. While at the hospital, I had also contacted Doris Mueller, our Swiss neighbor of pre-war days, and she kindly came once a week to see me. She brought with her fruit, cake, and cookies for the children, and you can well imagine how welcome these things were. She also brought some of my clothing that she had been able to rescue from the house, and a little canned food which proved a godsend. She promised to have the children's beds sent in when we returned to camp. While at St. Luke's, I shared a room with Mrs. Harrington, a woman who had permission to be there while her husband underwent, and recuperated from, an operation. He was the former British consul but was now retired.

They are such a nice couple, and it seems so sad to have people their age undergoing these hardships. They have lived in the East for such a long time and were about to leave for England to settle down quietly, but instead, they are being pushed about by the Japanese, and I only hope they survive this internment to see better days. Besides Stan Kingsbury, there was Ben Zwillig and Pablo Davis with whom I talked, and sometimes played bridge. Ben's birthday is October 18th, the same as mine, and we made a promise we'd have a wonderful party when the war was over. But the war still goes on, and poor Ben is gone. So is Pablo Davis;

they both died rather suddenly towards the end of last year. Stan is now at Los Banos.

While at the hospital we had a couple of bad earthquakes that shook the place terribly, and on another occasion, there was a lone plane that came from goodness-knows-where and dropped bombs at Parañaque. Rumor had it that there was a big conference of Japanese and German high-ups being held at the Los Tamaraos Polo Club; anyway, that place was destroyed, and we did hear that the house we used to live in at Tamaraos Court went with it, which would mean the end of our furniture there, if it had not been looted already. Perhaps we'll hear the truth later on. Personal possessions mean very little right now, when you consider the lives being lost in all this, so even though so many people have lost all their worldly belongings, as long as they can keep their health, they feel lucky. During my stay there, some of the women who were expecting at the outbreak of war, came to the hospital to have their babies, and later, to return to the camp with the little mites, and in many cases, just a handful of clothes and barely the essential food for them. After the war, there is a debt of gratitude I will gladly pay to a Filipino girl who didn't know me from Adam, but approached me one day at St. Luke's and asked me how I was making out with little things such as lipstick, etc. I told her my lipstick was almost gone and I didn't expect to get any more, but that our clothes were wearing fairly well; shoes were a problem, but I didn't intend to worry about such things as we would all be getting into a rundown condition together so I would have company. She pressed me to take ten pesos with which to buy some extra food for the children before taking them back to camp; I declined with thanks, but she seemed to wish me to have it so sincerely that I finally gave in. To my surprise, she arrived again the next day with a pair of shoes, a box of powder, a lipstick, and some buttons and thread, etc. I was so touched by all this that it really brought tears to my eyes. She said that she hoped we would all keep well, and that the Filipinos were all praying for the day when the war would be over, and we could all be released. We have so many kindnesses to remember from these people, and I hope in the excitement of being free again, our people will not forget them.

One of the biggest joys of being at the hospital was that we were able to take a hot bath each day—our first since January 5 1942, and now, goodness knows when we will get another.

Dr. Fletcher said that as we intended to return to Santo Tomas, it would be wise for me to have my tonsils removed at the same time as Ann's to avoid repeating the case of tonsilitis I had in March; so the day came when Ann was well enough and the doctor came from camp. I stayed with Ann until she was under the ether—such a horrid thing—then I waited on the porch until Eric arrived; he had obtained a few hours' release, so we waited until Ann was conscious, then he stayed with her while I went to the operating room. I just had a local anesthetic, so was back in my room in about twenty minutes. Eric had to leave then, and there followed an uncomfortable week for me, though Ann seemed to be alright in a few days. Six days after this, our pass was up, and as we could not get an extension, we returned to camp. I was given a space in Room 66 in the Annex—right opposite my old room—and the first thing that struck my attention was how much paler everyone looked. At this date, we were getting enough to eat, but it was such poor food and not really sufficient in vitamins, etc., that it made us feel that we were always hungry.

I naturally found many changes after being away so long.

A large piece of ground had been cleared by our men and vegetables were planted. While the entire camp could not be supplied, the Annex kitchen and the hospital were getting a good supply of these vegetables almost daily—mostly talinum, which is a leafy vegetable hated by all, some eggplant, and pechay. All these grow very quickly in the Philippines. There were organized sports, stage shows, lectures, school, classes, and Church services—all being conducted by people with experience. Permission had been given for internees to sit in certain areas outside until 8:15 p.m. instead of being indoors at seven as before. There was a music room where a camp broadcasting system was installed and records (loaned by internees) were played each evening. This cheered us up greatly.

Bataan had fallen in May, and later, the army nurses were brought into camp. At first, they were isolated in another building, but later on, the Japanese gave in and allowed them to mix with us. We needed nurses so badly for the camp hospital and no matter what they told us, there was nothing they could do about the war situation from there.

Concerning the package line—perhaps I had better go back to the beginning about this, as I haven't explained it properly—when we first came in, the Japanese were quite lenient in some respects, and the package line was one of these. At first, people outside were permitted to bring packages of food, to the front fence for us. Since the Japanese didn't intend to feed us themselves, it was about the only sensible thing they could do for us. The internees waited patiently inside to hear their names called; if you could get close enough, you might see your friend, servant, or relative through the bars, and many were able to pass messages this way. Different firms outside began catering meals which were sent to you in a native container called a fiambrera. This practice was allowed right up until the closing of the gate last January. After a short time, a space was cleared off and roped, so while you were able to see your party, you were not allowed to speak; but a censored note and money department was started so that you could send messages or money officially. Some people have had it comparatively easy, and I refer to those who had the sense to bring in a large amount of money, or knew just where to borrow it, or who had left some with, say, Spanish friends outside to pay their bills. These, of course were mostly just Manila people, and while they had plenty to put up with, it was much harder on the others. Their day would go something like this: right after breakfast (and at that time, the camp breakfast wasn't too terrible, and most of them ate it), they'd take soiled linen and empty food container down to the line, go back and clean up their space, perhaps do their camp work or just sit and talk or read; head down to the line again at 10:30 a.m. to pick up the fresh food and clean laundry left that morning. After lunch, they'd have a siesta, then go down to the line again to collect more fresh food for supper. After that meal, they'd sit out and listen to music or play cards. Later on, the afternoon package line was cut and things came in only once a day. They gradually allowed many things to come in that helped make life easier for some, such as electric irons and ironing boards, hot plates, percolators, non-electric ice boxes, beds, mattresses, cupboards, and cooking utensils; though during the second year they did confiscate all electrical equipment so that put an end to those little joys. The package line did help a great number of people, but I would say there was still two-thirds of the camp without any such assistance. Take ourselves—we came in with just a few pesos and for ages didn't know where to get more. When they permitted Filipino vendors to come in daily to sell fruits and vegetables, we stupidly sold canned food and clothes to enable us to buy some of these things, not knowing how much we would need them later. Take one item—when Johnny went to the Holy Ghost Convent, I sold a case of Heinz strained baby foods (thinking that he was getting too old for them and that he would get proper food there) for exactly what I paid pre-war—twenty-one centavos per can—and eighteen months later, after we were able to borrow money, I paid as much as three-pesos and fifty-centavos per can just to mix it with the terrible food to give it some nutrition. Lat-

er, all the fences were covered with sawali (a native, dried-leaf partition) and it was impossible to see people outside at all, so people gave up the practice of sitting near the gate for hours on end.I think I should mention, here, about the shanties—soon after we came in, permission was granted (for those who wished) to erect little shelters so they could spend the day away from the noise of the buildings and to eat more or less privately. Nipa, sawali, and bamboo were allowed in, and some people even bought good lumber. The majority, of course, turned up their noses at this foolishness and said that we wouldn't be here long enough to warrant such a thing. However, the others went ahead and built shanties. Some were content with four posts and a nipa roof to protect them from the sun. Others made quite sturdy places, similar to a traditional Filipino house. I remember when one party received the first complete nipa house from outside. This had only to be laced together with split bamboo threads and erected as per plan, and they had a nice cool house—on stilts—with split bamboo floors and nipa sides and roof.

Chairs, tables, and cupboards were sent from their home outside and they spent their days in comparative privacy. As the months wore on, this became quite a big thing and the campus was divided into districts with proper paths and named streets. Rules were made as to what hours you were allowed the use of your shanty. People began using Filipino charcoal stoves and did their own cooking. This was all very well for those who had the time, inclination, and materials available, but it certainly was hot, dirty work, and many wasted more energy trying to concoct something then they obtained from eating it. Later, when people began borrowing money from outside in earnest, the building of shanties increased, and some are really nice little places. While food was coming in more or less regularly, there was visiting back and forth and shanty life became quite a big thing. I rather envied this break away from the mass of other people, but at first, we not only couldn't afford to build, but thought it stupid. Later, when we could have borrowed, we decided with the children outside, we would make do and not run up debts unnecessarily, so all we indulged in was a wooden table to eat our meals at, and two folding chairs with two folding stools for the children. These, we purchased the first August, when we found, for the first time, time on our hands. Up till then, we never even had a chair to sit on. Until the rainy season started, we had been able to sit on the grass so the need didn't seem so great until everything became so wet.

When we returned from St. Luke's and I was offered the loan of an iron, it certainly was a nice civilized feeling to wear ironed clothes after six months of being rough and dry. Two weeks after our return to camp, I developed a bad attack of enteritis and poor Johnny commenced to have fevers off and on again. In July, when I was worried to death about him, a letter was posted on the notice board from Mrs. Adolph Ipekdjian (pronounced Ipekjohn), offering a home for six children under

three years of age, for the duration of our interment. She promised to feed, clothe, and look after them properly. I did not know the woman per-
sonally, but I knew of her. Her husband is a very
wealthy diamond merchant and city jeweler, and
their home is very nice. It was situated in the cool
section near where we lived in Quezon City, so I
thought deeply about this offer. Although I had decided not to part with the children, it was evident
that the camp was no place for Johnny. Ann made
out alright, but I didn't want to send Johnny anywhere alone. Finally, I decided to try it, at the same
time having in mind the idea of offering myself to
Mrs. Ipekdjian in any capacity at all so that I, too,
could get a pass from the Japanese to stay there
and be near the children. With this in mind, I listed the children's names. This was sanctioned by
the Japanese, and towards the end of July, I packed
up their things and together with four other kiddies, they departed. It was a hard break for me,
but luckily the children didn't fuss, so that helped.
Mr. and Mrs. Ipekdjian came in a car and were allowed by the guards to come inside the gate for a
few minutes. We were introduced to them (by one
of our people who worked in the office and was attending to details of the transfer of the children).
They seemed very nice and promised to take every
care of the children. The little ones thought it such
a great treat to go off in a car that there wasn't the
crying I had anticipated. I think Mr. Ipekdjian's

nationality is Armenian, and she was American before her marriage. The Japanese look on her the same as her husband, so that is the reason she is outside, though her sister, who is married to a British fellow, is here in camp with us. When the children had gone, I looked the sister up, told her my plans, and asked what she thought. She was very nice, but said she felt sure that her sister wouldn't want any parent there, partly because they had a large household already, and partly because if she did it for one, others would want to go too. I hadn't really thought of it in that way. She explained that besides Mr. and Mrs. Ipekdjian, there were Mr. and Mrs. Jones (the father and stepmother to Mrs. Ipekdjian), Maria, an elderly-but-capable Spanish nurse/amah who had taken care of them as children, a few Filipino amahs, cooks, and houseboys. She pressed me not to worry because they were all fond of children, and she knew they would do everything for them. In fact, Mrs. Ipekdjian had had three attempts to have a child herself, but had lost all three babies at birth and was very brokenhearted about it. It really was a lovely and unselfish thing she was doing, and such a responsibility too. Well, the next thing was to hound the office for permission to visit the children once in a while, or to have them brought in to see us. The Japanese, I thought, were quite reasonable about this, because they said the children could be brought in once every two weeks. The first two weeks naturally dragged, but the visiting day came, and I remember how we sat down near the gate waiting. At last, they came in and it certainly was a joy to see them. Mrs. Ipekdjian had little dresses and suits made for them, and they looked so cute. They all looked so clean and well cared for and were quite happy. Ann was able to tell us more or less accurately about the place. She said they had a nice bed each, a warm bath every day, and nice food plus two dogs to play with. This was a great relief to us. We gave them as nice a lunch as we could rustle up, then they had a siesta, and Mrs. Ipekdjian called for them about four o'clock. This was the time I had been dreading, but I needn't have worried because as soon as the children saw her, they ran to her and seemed even overanxious to go off with her. She assured me that Johnny, especially, had been quite well, and that they hadn't fretted after the first night. At this, I decided to leave them there because at such a time, my feelings could not be considered— the main thing was to keep the children in good health. This took care of the worry of the rainy season (which was well underway), when the children had previously gone through one very bad spell of about five days when they couldn't even venture outside the room. This was a worry, especially because of the laundry problem as nothing would dry. I loaned the children's cribs to parties who needed them. As I was then alone, I was forced to move into the main building. I finally got a space in room 30A on the second floor. This was a large room, and housed about fifty women. We were packed much closer together than in the Annex, but luckily, I was in line with a window so got some fresh air. I then had to think about camp work as I was now eligible for detail. They were badly in need of someone to look after the Annex vegetable cleaning, so I took this on. You see, up until and including this time, the women who cleaned vegetables for the main line didn't see why women with children should be pampered, so they refused to do extra vegetables for the Annex; therefore, we had to do our own, and as a mother's day was always full with laundry, standing in lines, and minding the children, we decided to do them in the evenings.

At eight o'clock each night—if your name was listed—you went to the dining room and peeled vegetables for usually one and one-half hours. My job was to find out from the cook what vegetable there would be for the next day and how much of it was needed, then taking into consideration how many paring knives were at our disposal, make an alphabetical list of names of the Annex mothers and post it on the same board around 7 p.m. I would go in and place the vegetables from the baskets along the dining tables in as many even bundles as there were women. When the women came on duty, I'd tick their names off the list, then go up and down the tables putting the pared vegetables into pans, then into large cooking pots, and collecting the peelings in another pan and placing them in the empty baskets for the garbage collectors. Each evening, I had to select two people per table to scrub the tables afterwards and sweep the floor. No one liked to do a speck more work than the next, so I had to watch that I rotated properly and didn't put anyone on more than another. There were many gripes, and lots of times I was there until ten or ten-thirty because some didn't show up for work. Eric didn't like me having this job because it meant I couldn't sit outside with him and listen to the music, but I felt I was doing the mothers a good turn, as they were too busy to attend to the organizing part of the job. Besides, sitting listening to the music, while pleasant, was rather upsetting at times and gave me too much time to think. I had only just started this job in August when I came down with dengue fever and spent ten days in the camp hospital. The children came in for their visit once during this time, and I was able to struggle down the stairs for a minute just to say hello to them. The day before I left the hospital, Eric came down with it and also spent ten days there.

Every day, during the months that followed until Christmas, I knitted frantically with this fine string that I had bought, making socks as everyone needed them badly, and it was a small source of income to enable us to buy fruits, etc. for the children's meals when they came to visit us. I also knitted a little pullover for each of the children, and I think when I finally ran out of thread and it was impossible to buy more, I had knitted thirty-eight pairs of socks, plus the other things, and I was quite tired of it.

In October, something was said about making Christmas more enjoyable for the children, but it died a natural death as no one wanted to admit that we would be there that long. During November, however, we did form a committee and got busy making stuffed toys for the children. Late in November, the Japanese permitted us to put on a Hobby Show, and this was a most interesting affair as everyone was amazed to see just how many really nice things had been made by the internees during their spare time. As some materials were difficult to get into camp, the art section seemed to be the most popular as it just took paper and pencil, and we have some really brilliant artists interned here.

Before I relate about Christmas, perhaps I should explain a little bit about the buying of goods. During March 1942, if you did not have contact with the outside, you were allowed to buy a few necessary items through a Spanish girl whom the Japanese permitted to come into camp once each week. It was through her that I bought thread. Eric laughed when I did it saying, "why, it is just the string they use to sew up the sugar sacks," but many women were buying it, and later, it certainly proved a godsend in crocheting bras, and knitting socks and sweaters. From one-peso fifty-centavos per cone, the price gradually rose until one cone cost 150 pesos. Then, finally, it was impossible to buy it at all. After this Spanish girl, they allowed the firm, Aguinaldos, to come in daily and operate a sort of order counter, where you ordered things one day, and collected them the next. This was a great boon to those who had some money, and their sale of folding chairs was terrific. As for food-stuffs, in the very first days, there were a couple of Indian fellows who had been employed by the University and were still on the property, and they sold small amounts of fruits and vegetables to us on the quiet. On March 2, for Eric's birthday, I bought a nice mango and a couple of tomatoes from them from our small fund—some birthday present. On February 26, for Ann's birthday, we hadn't heard of these Indians and had bought her some terrible local-made candy from the Japanese store where you could buy cigarettes and some canned food, though their prices were prohibitive.

Later still, a second Japanese-owned store opened where you could buy carabao (water buffalo) milk and ice cream, cake, and sometimes raw fish, meat, and eggs. Those who had money ate fairly well while this place operated, but of course, we couldn't use it often.

Towards the end of the year, the Japanese

allowed some Filipino vendors to come in each morning and sell fruit and vegetables, and they did a wonderful business. This was a great help to people to be able to get fresh things to eat, and we patronized them as often as we could. We didn't go all out like some people, and remember, throughout all this time, there have been a percentage of people who could not buy anything at all. To deliberately run up debts they knew they could not settle afterwards would have been foolish, and yet at the time of writing—which is now June 25 1944—nothing seems foolish so long as you can get enough to eat. Even going into debt for the next ten years. Because now, almost the entire 3,700 of us are constantly hungry, but I should leave that until I come to it.

As jobs seemed to become more numerous and varied, the Executive Committee began forming departments to take care of things. There was a Police Department which had to control rules such as: "no leaving the building before 6:30 a.m. or after 9 p.m."—these times have varied according to the whims of the Japanese; "no lights in any rooms after lights out"—in the earlier days not so much as a match could be struck, so if your child got sick and vomited, you just had to do the best you could in the dark. When they have practice blackouts for possible air raids, it is really miserable, and the police department has to keep an eye open for rule breakers. You see, we figured that if we took care that our own people followed the rules, that meant less interference from the Japanese. In the earlier days, there was the liquor problem. The rule read that "no intoxicating liquor should be brought into the camp" but the men in this country like their liquor, and they found many ways of obtaining it. They fooled the Japanese right and left in smuggling it in, but this didn't matter so much so long as the party took it carefully, because if there were no cases of drunks, then the Japanese wouldn't be so careful to detect it coming into camp. But of course there was always someone who would have to get under the influence and become noisy, and the police department was eventually forced to make a camp jail to put the offenders in. There was another rule that said the sexes must be separated, and that any public display of affection was prohibited; but once in a while of course, someone would be caught in their shanty after dark. Then, of course, there was thieving; yes, believe it or not, thieving goes on between internees. At the time of writing, I have to correct my previous statement that it was done by the bums of the camp, as I find that the more acute the need for food becomes, the more thieving is done, and often times by quite respectable-looking citizens. Just the same, this is quite a melting pot, and as I have heard it said, "they really had to scrape the bottom when they interned everyone." There are fellows who have done time in various countries. There are professional smugglers, beachcombers, and white men married to Japanese women and have settled down here, not that the latter are not respectable. They are interned, but their families—in most cases—are living outside, and although we help them with funds from the camp, it is still hard for them to get along, so it was found that all manner of things such as soap, toilet paper (before that luxury gave out), and clothing issued by the camp indigent section, were being smuggled out of camp to their families. One fellow (there were possibly more of them) had quite a system. He would help himself to good-looking clothes from the laundry lines—especially undies, which I am sorely in need of—and also my only wool blanket that Doris Mueller sent in for us, and a sheet. The day they caught this fellow, people who had lost laundry from the lines were asked to go to the police office to see if their things were among those retrieved from the package line, and I was lucky in getting back a blouse, a slip, and a towel.

To return to the other departments, there is the Sanitation Department which of course is so necessary in a place like this. Their work covers keeping ditches clear and mosquito breeding places under control, and garbage control—which has been a terrific thing and bears enlarging on. At first, everything was dumped in heaps and our men had to dig huge holes and bury it. For a camp of nearly four thousand people, you can perhaps

imagine how bad that was. At that time, the serv-
ings of food were quite generous, but the so-called
stews were so horrible in lots of instances that they
almost made us sick to eat them, and lots of it ended up in the garbage heaps. The odor was dreadful, and if you think garbage can smell in an ordi-
nary country, you just cannot imagine how bad it
gets sitting around all day without a cover under
the tropical sun. These details are not pleasant, I
know, but then nothing is in this place, so we may
just as well go into the nasty details. With constant talk, we managed to get permission for the
City Garbage Department to send in trucks, and
we were able to buy large bins to which we made
wooden covers, so for a long time, now, the garbage
problem has been taken care of. Of course, we are
now faced with the trouble that time has brought
on, and that is wear and tear on the bins. Many, I
think, were foolishly allowed to just fall apart. Now
we have an insufficient number left to cope with
the garbage, and the little material we have left
for mending such things is used for mending the
cooking pots, as that is, after all, the most important thing at this date.

While on unpleasant things and the Sanitation
Department, it might be just as well to talk about
bed bugs. You've probably heard of these things; I
had too, but had never seen one. Well, we hadn't
been here long before people began talking about
the worry of keeping free from bed bugs.

These vermin were certainly in the building before we took up residence, but the idea of having them in your own clothes, etc. didn't occur to lots of us because we thought we were too clean; however, we soon learned that you get them whether you are clean or not. In the early days when disinfectant was still available, you could go to the Sanitation Department and take out a flit gun full of the mixture, and armed with a cloth and a brush (if you were lucky enough to have one), you could take your mattress, pillow, and wooden bed out into the sun and get busy. Most people did this job once each week, but when you live upstairs it's just too much to get the things down and back, so the job is done only about every six weeks. Even Ann and John know what a bed bug looks like; they are certainly nasty pests to fight. They seem to be in all the University chairs, too, so it is nothing to get bitten every time you sit down. These days, with practically no disinfectant left, you must make do with boiling soapy water (if you can get it), and plenty of sunshine. The Sanitation Department has had various campaigns for cleaning the place up. On a few occasions, they issued plenty of fly swatters and got everyone interested in killing a certain number of flies each day; naturally, small boys took the job seriously and scores really mounted. Then they have rat and mosquito campaigns. They also started a good idea when they sent "inspectors" around every week to check up on the rooms. Each week, a certificate of award for merit is given to the cleanest room. This became something to work for, especially in the early days, when the reward was a tray of fudge; but shortage of materials (or rather ingredients) soon put a stop to that. It is much harder work to keep things clean today—with little, and very often, no soap; very few brooms (which are a native, soft variety); very little disinfectant; no flit; very few garbage cans; and so on . . .

Then, there is the Hygiene Department, the Construction Department, the Finance and Supplies Department, and the Recreation Committee.

During December, they reorganized work in the Annex kitchen, putting in a new cook and an entirely new staff of adults from the main building, which meant the mothers didn't have to prepare the vegetables anymore. This relieved me of my job, so I took on another one in the Annex Clinic. We are fortunate in having, besides the camp hospital, a clinic in each building, which is really necessary as traffic between buildings at night is prohibited. Permission must always be obtained from the Japanese when it is necessary for anyone to be taken to the hospital at night. The clinics just take care of smaller things, and as they need all available nurses for the hospital, the doctors on duty in the clinics just have a non-registered person to help them. For the first two years, they permitted two Filipino doctors to come in for night duty to relieve the strain on our few doctors, and the one I assisted in the Annex from six to nine each night was Dr. Jayme (pronounced Hymee). At the same time, I took on a three-hour morning job in the music room, keeping records and helping compile the programs.

Ann and John continued to be brought in to visit once every two weeks, and it was always such a pleasure to see them looking so well. They never fretted and had learned to care a great deal for their old Spanish nurse who never spoke English to them, but they all learned to understand her and could even say many things in Spanish. Early in December, we were permitted to write letters home—that is, one letter per family and only one page. I wrote as much as I could to you, Mother, but of course, have learned since that you never received it.

Later in December, the "enemy aliens" who had been interned in Cebu were brought into our camp, and I think despite discomforts, they were all pleased to be with such a big group.

About this same time, Red Cross food packages arrived, some being marked *South Africa* and others *Canada*. We were all pleased and surprised, and hoped they would be distributed in time for Christmas, but on this we were disappointed; we received them early in January, and it really was a treat to have some tasty things to eat after all the messy stews and native foods we have been having. I remember the long line that formed when we were told we could collect them, but this was a pleasure to stand in. We all looked like children at a party, and believe me, little cans of food never looked so good to us before. We decided to eat up the things we thought might perish, and to keep the rest as long as possible, but this was hard to do. Some people, especially those who received food daily from the package line, were able to hold their canned goods for a long time. We did manage to keep a few cans of corned beef for six months, but the more delectable items were polished off in three months, and we really enjoyed them all.

Taking everything into consideration, Christmas of 1942 was quite a festive time. We didn't dare plan too much for one day; spinning the "pleasures" out over a period of a week made the time seem quite gay. The children put on a pageant that was a pleasure to watch. Then one evening, we were allowed to see our first movie. But before the main picture was shown, we had to suffer through lots of Japanese propaganda films. Another evening, we listened to a lovely Christmas program put on by the mixed chorus. These men and women had practiced for several weeks, and their singing was a pleasure to listen to. One afternoon, there was a big softball game which was quite exciting, and another time there was a soccer match between England and Scotland. There were other items such as community singing and special church services. Then, on December 24, Mrs. Ipekdjian brought the children in to see us, and we gave them each a stuffed toy that I had made. I didn't mind them missing the camp celebration because they were to have a nice Christmas party at the Ipekdjian home.

On Christmas Day, the Japanese permitted near relatives of people interned to visit the camp for a few hours. This made the front grounds look very gay and gave those concerned much pleasure. There was a big package delivery that day, and to our joy, there were three packages for us. One was filled with good food from the SyCip family, another of food from Doris and Gene Mueller, and another from her with some extra items of clothing in it. These came in handy, and during the second year I would have been sorely in need of clothes without them as I had to cut so many of my things down for the children. We were sorry that the food would not keep long enough to save until the children's next visiting day; still they were getting good food at this time, so it would not have meant so much to them. We would take our precious packages out at each meal and eat some little thing from them and put the rest away. When I think back now on the mental picture of myself furtively tucking the packages out of sight between my suitcases under the bed in case some hungry person became light fingered, it seems laughable, but at the time, it was no laughing matter. In fact, it was dead serious to us, and I remember the real pain we suffered when we found the ants that had beaten us to the last piece of cake we were saving; however, at this stage, we removed the offending ants and enjoyed what was left.

The children in the camp really had a grand Christmas Day, the main event being the distribution of gifts in the afternoon. I had been a member of the Christmas Committee and we had really worked to see that the gifts were made in time. Each child received two gifts, and later they were all served cake and ice cream, fruit juice, candy, and cookies. Someone managed to send in a Santa Claus costume and this was worn by Dr. Mulchay, an Australian, who made a very good Santa. During the afternoon, the grounds fairly bristled with Japanese from the propaganda department, and they took many pictures of the children, their gifts, and the party. No doubt, these appeared elsewhere in greater-East Asia to show just how "kind and benevolent" the Japanese authorities were. On December 26, the American internees seemed amused at the British element celebrating Boxing Day, as this holiday is not known in their country. That evening, we had another movie so this was gaiety indeed.

1942 came to close, and after we received the Red Cross packages early in January, the next pleasure for me was more letters from home. It was lovely to read the news from home, but it bothered me that you were so worried on our behalf, yet I could not let you know that we were alive and well.

The first unpleasant episode to occur in 1943 was an order issued from the Japanese office concerning pregnant women. No doubt they thought ample time had been allowed for all babies conceived before the war to be born, and they were determined to punish those who had broken the rules, so all expecting women were made to pack immediately, and were sent to a Spanish old people's home (as I understand it), where they had to wait, and, once their babies were born, were granted permission to return. Meanwhile, the husbands or men responsible were lodged in the camp jail for a period of ninety days, while any existing children of those parents were sent out to the Holy Ghost Convent.

While I felt very critical of the adults concerned, there were a few cases where I felt just sick with pity that the children should be punished so. One case was a British man named Fernandez who had a Spanish wife. They already had two girls who spoke Spanish and were very unsure of any English. They were shy kiddies, and had never been parted from their parents before; naturally, they were just heartbroken about being sent away, and I was told by other parents who visited their children at the home that the two girls just fretted continuously.

Another case was Mrs. Nash, who had been

outside on a pass with her two children for some months during the first year and at times, her husband had managed to obtain a pass to be with them. Naturally, they didn't conform to all rules as in camp, but the Japanese didn't take that into consideration and separated them anyway. Mrs. Nash is a brilliant violinist and a charming person, and she was dreadfully upset over this. Her husband managed to get the two boys back to camp after he had completed his jail sentences, and it was lovely to see the way he tried to make up to them for the absence of their mother. This episode put a little fear into others, so things quieted down in this direction for the rest of the year.

The next unpleasant event brought to light one of those low types of people who carries information to the enemy. His name was Owens, and it seems he had brought trouble on himself by paying too much attention to another man's wife. Then, when he suspected he was in for some trouble with the irate husband, he gave himself up to the Japanese officials, explaining that he really was a member of the Armed Forces, and should be treated as a war prisoner rather than a civilian.

He then went a step further and told them that he knew there were others in the camp posing as civilians, and this information really set the Japanese off on a tangent. Orders were issued for such men to turn themselves in and the result was that nearly forty men were bundled into army trucks and taken out of camp. Rumors reached us that they were treated rather badly at Fort Santiago, and were later taken to various war prison camps. These men, I might add, were not deserters as you might have gathered, but mostly fellows who were perhaps off duty and unable to be reached at the time orders were issued to leave Manila. There were other reasons too, and I think that very few of them—if any—were actual deserters. Owens was one, as you will have guessed.

Several of these men had to leave wives and children in the camp, and being rather doubtful as to their fate, there were tears, and it was a very sad group of internees that watched those trucks pull out.

Another event in January was one that didn't bother us any but did cause a deal of inconvenience to shanty owners. There was an order that all shanties be vacated because internees had not been conforming to the rules as to just how they should be built. It was rather funny, really, to see little groups of personal belongings and native cooking equipment here and there along the walks and paths. Luckily, there were no heavy rains during the evictions, and very soon the majority were permitted to take up residence again while the remainder hastily made the necessary alterations to their shanties. Then they too moved their things back.

Throughout January, rumors also persisted that our camp, or part of it, was to be transferred elsewhere. This made us all restless and worried as to where it would be and how we would get on, so all in all, the new year didn't start very well for any of us, and we all tried to console ourselves by saying that we supposed we would have to expect it to get worse before it could get better. We didn't realize how right we were. During February, a camp canteen was opened along with a cold store department. Then a personal service counter opened where you could order something, and if possible, the buyers would purchase it outside and sell it to you with an added 10 percent charge, which was put into the camp funds. These three conveniences worked very well for those who had money, and just served to tempt those without to borrow. At best, it made them very miserable; however, it did help many to keep in a better state of health, so for that it served a good purpose.

The Japanese used to allow a small number of passes daily, the idea being, if you had good enough reason to leave the camp, you could do so within the hours of ten and four. The procedure was to fill in a detailed application and hand it in to the release department; if they knew, or thought they knew, that your excuse was good enough, then your name was placed on the waiting list to be given to the Japanese. I am not in a position to make exact accusations, but I do know for a fact that many reasons were just cooked up, and people got away with it. Then too, I firmly believe that popularity, and perhaps one's social standing, had a lot to do with the rapidity with which one's pass was presented to the Japanese. When I first learned that the officials were allowing women to go out to procure additional clothing for their children, I naturally filed an application asking to be allowed to go to our former home to see if I could rescue any clothes for Ann and John. This was in September of 1942, and I know of a great many people who applied well after I did yet received their pass in a much shorter time. I finally learned to pester the men on the release department daily, and I feel sure had I not done this, I never would have received a pass. As it was, I finally got it late in February of 1943, and at last, by exchanging with another party, I was able to go out on February 26, which is Ann's birthday. When out on a pass, one was supposed to go directly to their destination and come right back, but the Ipekdjian home was en route to our place, so I determined to call there and see the children. This was really quite a big event for me, and I couldn't have felt more elated had I won a lottery or something of the kind. I was made to wear a red armband with Japanese characters on it, like all others out on release and this made me feel very conspicuous. I left the camp at ten that morning, and had to bow low to the guards at the gate.

There I was on the big outside. I started walking right away and eventually a crowded bus came along, into which I managed to squeeze. In the bus, Japanese soldiers and Filipinos alike all stared at me, but I just looked them right back in the eye. From the main road, I had quite a long walk to the Ipekdjian house, and I felt very nervous at this time in case I should bump into a Japanese who might ask to see my pass. But I was lucky and reached the house safely. No one knew I was coming on this day, so they were very surprised. It was lovely to see the children in such normal, peaceful surroundings, and they seemed so happy. Mrs. Ipekdjian was very kind. She showed me all over the house and told me how the children spent their days. She had had the upper floor furnished with small beds and a big table with small chairs, or rather, I should say a long table, and everything looked very comfortable. I couldn't stay long as I still had some distance to go, so Mrs. Ipekdjian kindly called a caratela and off I went. (cart)

I arrived by noon and went straight to Doris and Gene Mueller's house. They were surprised and pleased to see me and insisted that I have lunch with them. This was quite an event to sit at a proper table on a nice chair and eat nice food with good cutlery. In fact, I felt so awkward and overwhelmed at it all that I badly wanted to cry. Doris still had a servant, and he waited on us at the table just like old times. She told me how she had rescued a trunk from our house and filled it with whatever she could find at the time, hiding it in her basement. This was a great risk as she doubted the sincerity of her servant, and the Japanese would severely punish any neutral found harboring enemy possessions. I felt rather guilty in allowing her to continue minding it, but she insisted. I told her if at any time she thought trouble may be brewing, to get rid of it—burn it or throw it in a ditch or anything. I learned afterwards that within the next few months, her servant threatened to report her. She fired him, then put the trunk back in our basement. Nothing happened for several months, then she heard that the Swiss people occupying the house were being ordered out, and that some Japanese authors were moving in. She and Gene took a chance once more and transferred the trunk back to their basement, and they got by with it.

Doris bundled up several things that would come in handy to us in camp including a few of my washable dinner dresses that were overlooked by whoever looted our belongings.

Out of these, later on, I had clothes made for the children. She also gave me homemade jam, sausage, cake, and fruit. Oh what luxuries they were! She then came with me to our former home and introduced me to the occupant. It hurt quite a bit to see these people in our place, and I felt so envious—even of the nicely polished and carpeted floors compared to the hard concrete at the camp. I felt sure these people were afraid to even have me in the house in case of a visit from the Japanese wherein they could be accused of assisting the enemy. I was not allowed further than the porch—they offered a weak excuse about some member of the family taking a nap.

When I asked about our clothing, the woman insisted there was nothing left when she took up residence, and it was clear to me that she couldn't get rid of me quickly enough. It made me feel like someone with a contagious disease, to be spurned so by a white person.

I left Doris and Gene after hearty goodbyes; perhaps they were scared too, but they didn't let their fear alter their helping a friend, and I felt very grateful to them. I was laden with packages, and it was a long hot walk to the bus. During the drive back to the camp, the furtive glances of the Filipinos made me feel that it would be better to be in Santo Tomas after all. It was hard to say whether the glances spelled dislike, or whether it was that they had learned not to have dealings with whites—at least in public. I would not blame them if they did hate us quite a bit, because the majority of the Filipinos had such faith in the United States and her power to drive out, or rather keep out, the enemy. And they had been badly let down, having lost thousands of their people in a hopeless battle. And while the Japanese occupied their country, they had to suffer at their hands and live in constant fear of what was going to happen next.

I bowed low again to the guards on my return to the gates, and waited while my packages were searched. Then I went back inside the four grey walls of Santo Tomas, having seen all I would see of the great outside for another two years. I returned my armband and official pass to the office and thanked the Japanese in charge for allowing me out, and that was that. The food that Doris had given me made the next few days very pleasant, and had it not been the tropics, we could have kept it longer. During February and March of 1943, the rumors about the Japanese losses in the south were very persistent. Of course, the local paper, which they were still allowing in the camp at the time, insisted that the "entire Pacific Fleet" had been sunk, and that they would be invading Australia very soon. But we always managed to read between the lines. For instance, one day the paper would speak of a battle at such and such a place and how they had sunk so many and put the enemy to rout, then in a short time, we would notice in the paper that they—the Japanese—were bombing the American positions in that same place, so it was only too clear to us what had really happened. That helped to cheer us a lot.

It was a lucky thing for me that my pass was not delayed until early in March, because one day, for no apparent reason, the Japanese Military Police cruised about in trucks picking up anyone they saw with an armband on. They would not listen to reasons or explanations but instead took them all to Fort Santiago, the very name of which place we almost whispered on account of the dreadful things we'd heard went on there. There, our people spent a very uncomfortable night and day, but were finally brought back to camp. The exception was two men who were considered to be "out of bounds," and they were given jail sentences.

One of these men, whose nickname was Leftie, used to be in the same room as Eric. He was charged with not wearing his armband. After his sentence was completed, he returned to camp, but it was impossible to get him to say a word about his treatment at Fort Santiago. It was generally known that when anyone was allowed to leave there, they were threatened with terrible things if they ever spoke of what went on in that place. Later in the year, I did have a talk with Mr. Roy Bennett and he didn't seem to be afraid to say just what he thought. Mr. Bennett was, or used to be, the managing editor of the Manila Daily Bulletin, and before war broke out, he used to air his opinions in his editorials in a very frank manner. The result of his outspoken attitude was that the Japanese made him a prisoner just as soon as entered Manila.

Our home had been on a hill that overlooked their place, and so often I used to admire his beautiful garden. I would see he and his two little daughters puttering about in it and giving instructions to their gardener, and they looked to be such a happy family. But all that came to a sudden end. What he suffered at the hands of the Japanese for the next eighteen months makes horrible reading. When they finally permitted him to return to the camp, he had to be hospitalized for some considerable time. In fact, I think he was still receiving treatments at the end of the internment. To learn more of the heinous ways the Japanese treated their prisoners, I would advise reading the chapter "Fort Santiago—an Oriental Inquisition" in the book *Santo Tomas Internment Camp* written by Frederic H. Stevens.

He was a prisoner there for many months, and knows of what went on.

May 1943 was an unhappy month for many. The Japanese announced that our camp was to be transferred to a place called Los Banos, but as it turned out, the entire camp never was transferred. First, they selected eight hundred men to go build barracks, and with them went our small contingent of navy nurses—twelve in all. The next day, the local paper carried an article about it on the front page. It told how "through the kindness of the Japanese Authorities, a trainload of happy internees were transferred to a new home in the country; smiling and eager children were seen waving from the windows and waiting for the first glimpse of their new pleasant surroundings." What a lot of bologna, as an American would say. What really happened was that they were all herded into boxcars from which they couldn't see a thing. They were generally treated like animals—the nurses too—and of course there weren't any children sent at that time. Well, that's the way it goes. The Japanese allowed these eight hundred men some lumber and told them to build large enough places to accommodate a few thousand people. They said when they were complete, they would allow the wives, children, and some other internees to go to Los Banos. We used to hear through the grapevine that things were very hard for them during the first months. There was said to be a shortage of water, and they had to carry it from quite a distance away. Our friend Martin Craven was one of the eight hundred, and naturally, Louise was anxious to join him.

Right after this event, the Japanese began tightening up on all the rules, and we wondered if perhaps they had received some serious setbacks on their fighting fronts. They recalled hundreds of people who were living outside on so-called permanent passes—that is, they had been told their excuse was enough to permit them to live away from the camp for the duration. When the children were allowed to go to Mrs. Ipekdjian's place, it was understood it was also for the duration, so when we were informed that they would be returned to the camp within the week, we became very excited. We felt sure that trouble was about to begin for the Japanese, and we thought it would probably be only about another three months before the Americans were in Manila. What optimism. People came in every day of that week, and the housing committee had their troubles trying to find space for everyone. Due to the cramped conditions, the Japanese finally permitted some of the men who had shanties to use them during the nights, so there was quite a rush to be on this list, as the idea of sleeping away from the masses, regardless of the type of shelter, naturally appealed to many. At that time, there were many who wished they had a shanty too.

There were many mothers and children returning to camp, so there was quite a re-shuffle of rooms. Men were moved from the second floor of the main building, and this was made a women's floor—half for mothers and children, and half for the rest. I happened to be very fortunate here, because I was allotted to room number thirty-two, and this was a room where the male occupants had pooled together to put in screens in the early days. They kindly left the screening up, whereas the men from the only other screened room were angered at having to move out, and so took all the screens down. It was certainly wonderful not to have to sleep under a net, especially as getting up and attending to the children at night was always a bother when nets had to be tucked in again in the dark. Invariably, in the morning, you would find you had let in a few mosquitos. Well, I had the children's cribs returned to me, and I washed and sunned them thoroughly and had our space all ready when the children were brought in to camp. Mrs. Ipekdjian came with them and tried in vain to get the authorities to change their minds as she wanted so badly to keep them with her, but the answer was a firm *no*, and she actually cried when she said goodbye to them. I might add here that she seemed to be rewarded somewhat for her kindness, because towards the end of the year, she did have a baby of her own. When we left Manila for the States, the baby was quite well and doing fine and both she and her husband were very happy, but I will add more about these people before I am through.

At this time, we were wiser in the ways of other internees compared to when we first arrived in camp, so as soon as I was told what room I was to move into, Eric and I just hung about the corridor like flies, watching intently until the previous occupants moved their tables from along the wall. Then we pounced on what looked to us to be the best spot, right opposite the door, and by a window overlooking the patio. Here, we placed our homemade table and the stools we had scrounged from about the University. This made an excellent place to have our meals and to sit when doing nothing else. It saved taking the children down to the public dining sheds during the rainy season, so altogether we were much more comfortable than in the early days. Doris had sent in some bedclothes, so at least we did have a bed each—a mattress and bedclothes—and a space where we could sit and talk by ourselves. The rainy season held no terrors for me in the main building as it did in the Annex, especially as we were on the second floor. It was wonderful to have Ann and John back with us, though naturally we hated for them to have to live again in those unnatural surroundings.

There were nine mothers and fourteen children in room 32, and some of these women hadn't been in camp before so didn't know what-was-what about many things. They didn't know, or perhaps couldn't imagine, how bad things had been before, so it made me rather bitter when they grumbled so much and refused to take their turns at this and that. Also, at the time, people were borrowing money in large sums and paying others who were less fortunate to do their chores for them. Their attitude was "why do it when I can pay to have it done?" But this didn't seem altogether right to me—to pay money for labor when it seemed everyone should use it for food or medicine while those items were still for sale. The rest of the women elected me for Monitor of the room, and while I thought this job should be done by one of the mothers with only one child, I accepted, rather than have one of the new arrivals take the job and start imposing unfair rules on the rest of us. It seemed to me that throughout the buildings, Monitors were generally much too bossy and it made the place more like a jail; they posted rules all over the walls and woe betide anyone who broke them. I had quite a bit of experience in room 30A where the Monitor was just like you might expect a police-woman to be, so I decided then and there that we wouldn't have rules posted anywhere. I would pass the rules around to the women as I received them, and when they had digested them, I'd put them way out of sight. This seemed to work very well and friends visiting our room used to remark how nice and homey it looked in comparison to others. Generally speaking, the group remained congenial and we all got along fairly well; in fact, had I met the same group socially before the war, I'm sure I would have been happy to have all of them as friends.

Early in June there was a severe typhoon that kept the kids confined to the room and halls for a whole week. Eric and I had to go out in the rain each mealtime to stand in line for our food. There was no hope of doing any laundry and getting it dry, so when we ran out of clothes, we just had to wear the dirty ones. The week after this, Johnny tripped on the leg of the wood screen that stands outside our bathroom door and cut his chin badly; in fact, it bled so much that I didn't stop to see how bad it was, but put a couple of towels around his neck, picked him up, and rushed to the main floor clinic. The doctor on duty told me to take him to the hospital, which meant a long trek across the grounds. My, did he feel heavy! The doctor there cleaned up the cut and instead of stitches, put a clamp on it, then gave him an anti-tetanus shot, all of which Johnny didn't like. I felt pretty sick myself. He had to wear this clamp for a week, so you can imagine how anxious I felt with this metal thing sticking on the point of his chin. I was scared he would knock it off, especially as he usually sleeps on his stomach. However, it was alright, and the wound healed quickly.

Late in June, Eric and I finally decided to borrow some money as the food was getting terrible and there was not enough to satisfy anyone. It was just too much for us to see Ann and John go hungry while others were buying fresh fruits and vegetables from the vendors. We had gone the first eighteen months without borrowing any, and I hoped borrowing wouldn't be necessary at all. Prices were soaring sky-high, and money didn't go far. But the few extras we were able to buy helped a lot.

No doubt, you are wondering who we were able to borrow money from. Well, since prices were soaring and the only money allowed to be used was Japanese "Mickey Mouse" currency (as it was commonly called), a lot of people on the outside—especially the Chinese—were piling up stacks and stacks of it. These people suspected that when the Americans came back— and by now, they felt sure the Americans were on their way—the Japanese money would be useless. Thus, they were anxious to get rid of it, and they figured that an IOU from an internee for good American dollars was a good bet. The rate of exchange was absolute robbery, but they were anxious to lend, and we were anxious to eat, so there you are. Some people who had been in the employ of large firms and who knew, or felt sure, they would be paid their back wages when the internment was over, borrowed large amounts as often as they could. Eric, being an independent salesman, knew he could not count on any of the firms he sold for to reimburse him anything, and for this reason, he tried to avoid borrowing. I might add here that we only borrowed after we felt really sure that the government intended to help us all when we were released. Outside, a rumor had persisted for many months that people had heard on American radio reports that those of us who were interned would be paid at the rate of a dollar per day for our interment. At first, this sounded too good to be true, but gradually we came to believe it, and it was on the strength of this that we borrowed. Of course, we have since learned that it was entirely false, and the best we can hope for is that some day in the dim distant future, the government may get around to settling the many claims that we have been told we may file against losses. In the meantime, we remain in debt up to our ears in money that we were almost forced to borrow to buy food to help keep us alive. It does seem to me that since the US government had intended to send supplies of bulk food for the internees (only the Japanese refused to allow it), that some payment could be made to us to help in this regard. Well, I may as well bang my head against a brick wall as discuss it, so I will continue with my tale.

During July, John caught a very bad cold. That doesn't sound important enough to make a note of, but this was really a bad one and I was afraid of pneumonia as he couldn't seem to breathe properly—he just wheezed so loudly that you could hear it two rooms away. I called the doctor once in the middle of the night because of it, but he said there was nothing he could do, and he thought he would be alright. I remember how upset I was that the doctor wouldn't seem to do anything for the child, but now I recognize that John's cold was being caused by his enlarged Thymus gland. I didn't know he had such a gland at the time, but since we have been back in the United States, John has had two attacks, and the doctor here said they were caused by an enlarged Thymus gland. These attacks are very often fatal, so we can be thankful that John came through that one as well as he did.

During July, we had such bad weather—floods and winds of typhoon force—that it was agreed to take up a collection to enable a playhouse to be built for the children so that they would be able to run about and play even if the weather was bad. This was subscribed to by all who could manage it, and when the weather cleared, a site was selected not far from the back entrance to the main building, and work was commenced.

It was during July that we first heard of a list being compiled of people to be repatriated. This really caused lots of excitement and plenty of false rumors. It was the main topic of conversation for over a month. Finally, toward the end of September, a group of over one hundred internees left the camp in army trucks on the first leg of their trip home. We were all up early to see them off, and while we envied them, we didn't feel too bad because with our usual optimism, we felt sure that this was only the beginning, and that within a few months we would all be taken out. There were a lot of hard feelings about who on earth could have compiled the list of people to leave at that time, but I suppose it originated in Washington and was made up of people who had powerful allies in the States to pull strings for them. What seemed unfair to us was that we felt the young and able-bodied should have been left behind to permit the sick and aged to go first, but it was not to be, and many of the sick and aged died before being released.

Early in September, the playhouse was formally opened and it really looked grand. It was made of the usual bamboo with nipa roof and sawali sides, *woven mat* but it looked quite serviceable and cool. It did help the mothers a great deal, especially after someone was appointed to be in charge and she, in turn, appointed helpers so that there could be organized games, etc.

About this time, I received more letters from you, Mother, and a little later we were permitted to write our second letter. So I sent another to you, and as each adult was permitted to write this time, Eric sent his to John and Connie Ashley in Honolulu (since we had learned from your letters that both Mildred and Ethel had gone to the mainland). He asked if they would do us a favor and sell our furniture, etc. which was in storage, and deposit the money in our account at the bank. To have had this amount to come back to would have helped such a lot, but apparently the letter never reached them and when we returned, we had a storage bill that was too high for us to meet. We have heard, since our return, that Connie passed away that year, and we felt very sad. She and John were such a nice couple; they were pleasant company.

During this year, private enterprise grew in leaps and bounds. I'm sure it would have been better for all concerned if this had never been permitted. The camp canteen with a percentage going to camp funds was a much better idea, but permission was granted for individuals to operate, so those who had contact outside and could think of something they could make money on, went into business. Eventually, four or five rows of dining sheds were partitioned off. Sawali divisions were made and each person who applied for a vendor's license was allotted a space in what we termed "Robber's Row." John Hunter, a friend of ours from pre-war days, obtained permission to operate a restaurant, and this proved a wonderful brain child. Of course he worked hard, but he apparently had good contacts outside and seemed to have either pull with our guards on the inside gate, or with the Japanese guards on the outside gate, to say nothing of the release department, because he obtained permission to go outside on so many occasions that it must have been a great help to him. His restaurant was very popular with anyone who had any money—in fact, several who were borrowing regularly just gave up eating on the line and became regular customers of John's. I'm sure he must have made quite a decent amount out of this, but being a good salesman, he always cried poor.

During September, our John became sick again—the usual intestinal troubles with fever and lack of appetite. This grew worse, and the reliable methods failed to correct it. The doctor ran several tests, and while nothing showed positive, Dr. Jayme felt convinced it was dysentery and ordered the usual treatment. These injections are very strong, and in John's weakened condition, I didn't feel I should take chances, so after the first one, I took him to Dr. Fletcher with a copy of his blood test. This showed a very high infection and he thought it seemed like worms. There were such a number of cases of worms that it wouldn't have been surprising. Dr. Fletcher suggested putting him in the hospital for observation, so I agreed to bring him in the next day.

After worrying about it that evening, I finally went to see Dr. Jayme again and told him what I had done, and the outcome, and told him that as the child seemed to be going down so rapidly, I just had to have something done fast. John's weight had dropped six pounds in a little over a week. Well, Dr. Jayme was rather upset that I wasn't continuing with his orders, but he said he would test the whole thing. So, before he left the camp the next morning, I gave him a specimen. He smuggled it out; he was very often searched and was supposed to come and go empty handed. He took this to two leading parasite specialists downtown, and without knowing what the other said, they both diagnosed the trouble as "nutritional diarrhea," so Dr. Jayme got them together and told them of the exact symptoms and that he had made an error, and they kindly wrote out a diet and prescribed medicine for such a case.

I might add here that Dr. Jayme is quite young, and apart from emergency work during the Japanese bombing early in the war, this was really his first big responsibility. He was on night duty at the camp for two years and did a wonderful job, and I don't feel badly about his wrong diagnosis. When he came into camp the next evening, he told me what had happened and by much planning and kindness on his part, he agreed to help out with the diet. I was able to procure the medicine through the personal service canteen, but John had to have milkfish too, so the doctor made a deal with one of the Filipino fruit vendors to smuggle it in, and we picked it up while buying vegetables. The diet also called for buttermilk and to get this, Dr. Jayme enlisted the aid of a couple of friends who spent two full days trying every store in Manila. Finally, they located one can of powdered buttermilk, which seemed to be the last one left in town. This cost the enormous sum of forty-five pesos. Then there was a charge of fifty pesos for some Bl injections, which we were also able to get through the personal service canteen. All this meant we had to borrow more money, but this time we did it without hesitation. I think Dr. Fletcher must have thought me crazy because I just told him that I was watching John closely myself for a few days. Well, I did that too, and adhered strictly to the diet and medicine. We had to buy a Filipino charcoal stove (like people used in the shanties) to cook the fish and other things in tin cans, and do you know that within the week John had snapped out of it, and seemed quite alright. He had even started to gain some weight. I will always feel that Dr. Jayme saved John's life by his kind act, and I asked him to thank the two doctors outside for me, neither of whom would take a centavo in payment.

The 1943 rainy season was a long and severe one, and our nerves became very ragged during it. Day after day would be just the same, and while

Eric and I shared the jobs of standing in line for food, the children just lived from their room, to the bathroom, to our table in the corridor. Some days, of course, they were able to go to the playhouse. But there were days and days on end when it was too wet to even let them venture that far. You might think that so many children could play together nicely but it seemed impossible. They tired of their few toys and would quarrel easily on account of always being hungry. Some mothers were selfish in that they would go off someplace else to talk to other adults and leave their children to make as much noise as they liked. No doubt, I became selfish too, but I just couldn't stand the noise. So I got into the habit of taking just my two off. I would read or talk to them to keep them amused but if even one other child were to butt-in to hear too, I would become nervous and cross and would have to send them away. Many times, I used to think if I had to go through another rainy season, I would go out of my mind.

About the middle of November, there was a terrific storm. It was really a typhoon though the center of it, luckily, was some distance away. To give you some idea of the rain, twenty-seven inches were measured in three days, and I just can't tell you how severe the wind was. It howled for days and the grounds became so flooded that water was right up to the doors of the main building. All lines for food had to form inside, and there was such a jumble of people in the corridors at meal-times that it sounded like bedlam. Many shanties were blown down, while others flooded to such an extent that personal belongings—and even private supplies of rice and sugar—just floated away. When we asked a few of them why they didn't bring their belongings to the main building, they answered that when the water started to creep up, they piled their supplies as high as they could away from the floor thinking it was a sufficient precaution. Then they came to the building themselves to keep dry, and when they returned to their shanties thirty-six hours later, in many cases, the water was almost to the roof and the occupants had to visit what was left by raft. Up until this date, we had been allowed the use of gas and electricity in the main kitchen, but with the typhoon raging at its worst, both these powers were cut off and we were told they wouldn't be turned on to cook the next day's meals.

This really faced us with a problem, but a group of men headed by Charlie Kurz—the boss of the emergency crews—got busy, and when their plans were made, about nine or ten that night, they put their plan into action. The Japanese sanctioned this, of course, so they didn't have to worry about being on the grounds after hours. They cleared away about six or eight of the dining benches nearest the back door, and with water lapping about their ankles they started the rough foundation for an outdoor kitchen. I don't know how many men were on the job, but they worked in relays all that long wet night, bringing handcarts of huge adobe stones from a pile near the back gate (perhaps a distance of two hundred yards), then these were tossed chain-style from the pile where the boys dumped them to the other workers, and these they fitted into place. There was no time to mix cement to hold them, but the men built the thing so well that it held without any. By about four in the morning they had it finished. Holes provided the necessary fire space below each of their six iron cooking pots. Another group of men started the fires and got the water in the pots boiling, then the mush cooks came on and had the food cooked by the usual breakfast time. A path had been made between the two rows of pots for the cooks to walk on to do their stirring. This job really impressed me, though the men just seemed to take it in stride, so to speak. I think it was a wonderful thing that the fellows could get together the way they did and finish such a job without a hitch. For a while after that storm, the outdoor kitchen lay idle. If not for use during other storms, then to have in case the Japanese became mean and disallowed our use of gas, it seemed wise to have a more secure option. So these units were torn down, and in a short time, a really first-class job was done. The men mixed cement and set the stones evenly, finishing off the whole thing with a covering of cement. We then used these pots for cooking rice only, while vegetables and anything else we were lucky enough to get was cooked inside. Later in 1944, the outdoor kitchen had to be used for everything, and it was hard and dirty work for the men, but like all other unpleasant jobs, it was done. Late in November of 1943 another Hobby Show was permitted, and the articles on display were better and more numerous than the year before. In fact, the Japanese officials who saw the show must have kept it well in mind, because later the following year they suggested that if we wanted more food, it would be a good idea for us to make many such articles and sell them outside, but we talked them out of that. The lack of materials to work with was our main argument.

Throughout November, there had been very strong rumors about Red Cross relief kits having been brought back by the Teia Maru, the boat that took internees to Goa late in September. On the last day of November, we knew the rumors were true because truckloads of cases with the Red Cross stamp were brought into camp and placed in storage until such time as the Japanese decided to let us have them.

After two weeks, they ordered our men to have the individual cartons carried out and lined up in rows on one of the campus streets. This had us puzzled and we all looked on from upstairs windows and other vantage points. Finally, after the thousands of small boxes were in full view, a group of Japanese officials complete with their oversized swords arrived on the scene. The soldiers, and later, our men, opened each box, and the Japanese began searching. With the first few, they destroyed the contents, poking their swords into cans of powdered milk and corned beef, and emptying packages of powdered soups on the ground. This wanton waste just made us see red, and everyone was muttering threats; however, after members of our Executive Committee appealed to the Commandant, and he in turn appealed to the Military, they did stop ruining everything, but continued their inspection and ordered all the packs of cigarettes to be removed. It seemed that on the packages of Old Gold Cigarettes, there was printed a small Victory slogan and this, the Japanese took exception to. Eventually, this search came to an end, and to our surprise and pleasure, it was announced that the kits would be distributed immediately. There were enough for everyone to have a full kit and oh, what excitement there was everywhere. I remember we opened ours one by one and even took an inventory of the contents. We pored several evenings in a row into deciding how to best use everything, what would keep, and how long we could possibly make it last. Some people showed great strength of mind in keeping their boxes intact for several months, though one man in that group later died of starvation. When asked by the doctor why he hadn't used the food in his kit, he had replied that he was keeping it for worse days.

Having children, it was hard to resist their pleas for something else to eat, so we began nibbling at the kits right away. One precious item was Klim powdered milk, of which we each received four one-pound cans. That meant sixteen pounds for our children. We rationed this out to them at a glass a day and it lasted several months. We were so happy to see them get good milk after months of either none or a small portion of carabao milk. In turn, Eric and I gained the cans of powdered coffee from the children's kits as that was no use to them. Later, the packages of cigarettes were doled out to us, minus the Old Gold brand, of course, so Eric was lucky because he got my share too. They were not issued to children, though originally there were cigarettes in every kit meaning Eric would have received four shares; however that was his bad luck.

During December, a large group of women, some men, and children were sent to Los Banos, and Louise Craven was with this group. Despite the fact that they knew life was more difficult there, they were all happy to be going because most of them were joining husbands or relatives.

Toward the end of December, Red Cross bulk supplies of clothing and medicines arrived in camp. They were stored and, as with the food kits, the Japanese inspected these articles too. Eventually, they OK'd it, so the medicines were transferred to the hospital, while much time had to be spent in deciding the fairest way to distribute the clothing to the internees. There was enough of some articles for everyone to receive one, while in other things we were given a choice. Everything was greatly appreciated, and we felt quite ritzy with all our new things. New toothbrushes and tooth powder were especially cherished. The "Mother Hubbard" night dresses we women received were the funniest things in shape and size, and we called them our pup tents. However, one of the ladies in room 32 was an excellent seamstress and she fashioned hers into something very attractive and nice fitting, so with her advice, the rest of us followed suit. We used to feel that the ladies of our room looked quite smart going to bed.

Christmas week of 1943 was fairly gay, though not entered into with such enthusiasm as the one the year before. There was excellent singing of religious tunes by the women and children's chorus, and another evening "The Messiah" was presented by a chorus of one hundred and fifty internees. It was wonderful to listen to. On Christmas Eve, we were permitted a movie. This was most enjoyable because we hadn't had a movie in several months. Christmas Day was very similar to the previous one though not quite as well organized in my opinion, and if I remember rightly, the giving of the gifts to the children was something of a scramble and many children received more than others. Ann and John didn't show much enthusiasm about it all but enjoyed the day.

Right after Christmas an order that all vendors had to cease operation was issued, and this made the majority of us very pleased because their wares on display only served to make one more dissatisfied since their prices were so prohibitive as to be out of reach to all but a few who seemed to have a never-ending supply of money.

The next blow that fell concerned the package line, and of course this didn't bother us any as we had long since given up expecting any packages. We knew that conditions were beginning to get rugged outside as well; however, the group of people who were still receiving things from outside, and who still had their laundry done for them, were greatly put out at this turn of events. On the whole, though, we all looked at these drastic changes as a step nearer the end, because by now, rumors reached us of the losses the Japanese were receiving in the southern waters. We knew if they had been winning the war, if anything, they would have become more lenient with us.

1943 came to a close with a Walt Disney movie the night before New Year's Eve and this helped to lighten our spirits.

A pantomime "Cinderella" was put on by a teenage group the evening of January 1, and Ann and John really enjoyed this show. They talked about it for weeks afterwards.

The day after that, the people who had been interned in Davao were brought into camp, and there was a great bustle to make room for them. I think almost everyone in camp was out on the front plaza to see them arrive as many were friends and relatives of Santo Tomas internees. One woman I knew was so excited, she could hardly contain herself. It seemed that she had lived in Davao and a few months after the birth of her third child, she made the trip to Manila to have an operation, leaving her husband with the children. While recuperating before her return, war broke out, and she was caught in Manila and eventually brought to Santo Tomas. She never knew how her husband and children had fared until many months later when she heard through the grapevine that they had been interned too. Finally, they arrived, and what a poor, starved miserable group they looked—filthy dirty, after spending nine days and nights in the rat-infested hold of a dirty old ship without a proper toilet or washing facilities, and scarcely any food. Anyone who knew someone in the group had to contain themselves behind a roped area until the newcomers were screened by the Japanese, and then I remember seeing this girl—and she was still a girl, an attractive redhead—run to her husband and children, all of them redheads too, and it was a very touching scene. The two little girls were taking good care of their little brother, who could walk but was being held on account of his mother not seeing him for over two years. Later, I learned that her husband had a chance to escape by submarine, but rather than take risks with the three children, he gave himself up to the Japanese. The little boy was nicknamed Rusty, and was the pet of the Davao camp. We all did what we could to help make these people as comfortable as possible, and soon they were just part of our community. Still, early in January of 1944, the camp buzzed with nervousness when we were advised that the camp had been placed under the direct authority of the War Prisoner's Department, and that we could expect some drastic changes. Naturally, we all wondered a little fearfully what these would be.

The first change was with regard to food. Until this date, the authorities had allowed varying amounts per person per month, and our selected buyers would scour the town for the best they could get for that money. This was a good arrangement because those men were able to buy extra with any money that happened to be donated, or they might receive more than their money's worth from a sympathetic merchantman. Well, this had to stop, and we were told that in the future, the Japanese would bring the food to us. They first promised to supply 766 grams of foodstuffs per adult per day with half that amount for children. This arrangement wasn't so bad, but the anxious part was whether they would keep their promise.

The next thing we noticed was that Japanese soldiers patrolled the camp regularly, and of course, we didn't like this at all; in fact, there seemed to be a guard stationed at every corner. The majority of these we could avoid if we saw them first, but the one stationed on the road to the hospital annoyed us more than all. We had to use that road so much, and of course, coming and going, we had to stop, bow low, return, and go on. To forget meant to have your face slapped.

From these days on, it seemed that the military authorities just issued one pestiferous order after another. They seemed determined to keep us aware that we were prisoners, and they told us they didn't know how long they would be able to feed us, and so insisted that another large tract of land be started as a garden, and each man was forced to do his share in this garden regardless of his other duties. The annoying part of this garden was that the Japanese themselves confiscated a large percentage of the fruits of our men's labor, and the men naturally hated to feel they were working to feed the enemy. One bright thing that occurred quite regularly during January and February (then just occasionally until June) was the sale of eggs and small loaves of bread. At this time, any purchases had to be made through the group system that was, in effect, a canteen card with a number issued to every six adults. We were allowed one egg per person when they came in, and they gradually rose in price from eighty-five centavos to Pl.SO each. Carabao milk rose to P2.50 per pint and with these prices, we weren't able to buy very much. The bread that I spoke of was just a rice flour bread and was very poorly made. If you saw such a loaf today, you would immediately throw it out. These loaves were quite small and when they did come in, they were rationed at two loaves for every six people, or a third of a loaf each, and this amounted to very little.

After repeated requests for more doctors for the camp, the Japanese authorities transferred three of them from a War

Prisoner's camp. They were Dr. Noell, a general surgeon; Dr. Bloom, an eye, ear, nose, and throat specialist; and Dr. Francis, a dentist. All held the rank of Captain at the time. We were very thankful for the service these doctors gave the internees. Both Dr. Noell and Dr. Francis had wives in the camp, so they were fortunate indeed to be able to join them after such a long break.

Early in March, many people were lucky enough to receive packages from home; though, if I remember rightly, these came only from the United States. All the internees had a questionnaire to fill in a while after this, and I wonder now just how many we did fill in during the internment. It seemed like every few months they wanted to know all about you. Some questions even went as far as "What was the correct address of the place you were born: state, street, and number." They also asked where our grandparents were born and what their names were. Several times, they asked what our opinion was to the outcome of the war and why. We certainly had to do some head scratching to know how to answer some of them.

On March 11, it was announced that there would be a practice blackout from sundown to sunup. While it was awkward groping about in the dark, we didn't mind a bit because a real air raid would be just what we had been waiting for.

The food served to us during these weeks was so poor that we simply had to open up food from our private supplies. It almost seemed that the Japanese resented us having those Red Cross kits and were making things so tough that we would have to use them up.

It was announced, about this time, that in future we would be permitted to send one twenty-five word card per person per month to our relatives, though I now doubt if they ever bothered to send any of these on.

Quoting from my notes, March 23, I made rather a humorous entry to the effect that I was trying to explain what a beach was to Ann (she had forgotten), and I said one day we would visit one after the Americans came and released us. And she said, "Oh Mummy, don't be like Jimmy Green, always making up things." She had really forgotten that any other life existed, and naturally, Johnny didn't remember any either.

Perhaps it would be more interesting to quote exactly from my notes: Friday March 31: "To try to describe last night . . . For the first time in weeks I sat up late talking to other women until 11 p.m. At 12:30 we were awakened by Ad. Brunner's voice over the camp radio. 'All internees are ordered by the Commandant to remain in their rooms or shanties until further notice.' I thought of a possible air raid, but all the lights were on in Manila so that was out. Soon the voice again 'Turn on all room and hall lights and stand in a row near your doors for a roll call.' Children were permitted to remain in bed, thank goodness. Presently, along came a positive contingent of Japanese, the outside guards with fixed bayonets (I thanked my lucky stars Ann and John were good sleepers), interpreters, and members of the committee—Caroll Grinnell, Earl Caroll, and Sam Lloyd—and two MPs with unbuttoned revolver holsters. They came in and counted us, peered at the sleeping children, then went on their way. When they had completed the entire camp in this way, we were informed we could turn out the lights, so, consumed with curiosity, we returned to bed. At breakfast, I heard that they had spent till nearly six in the morning searching the fourth floor, so up to now we can only guess. Rumors are flying thick and fast this morning."

April 2 "A further list of 531 names were posted to be transferred to Los Banos. The evening
blackouts are still in effect, and all cooking in shanties has been prohibited. All electrical equipment
has been confiscated. The Japanese are really getting meaner, and roll calls are now much longer."

April 5 "We had to stand in line for a roll call
that lasted one and a half hours this evening.
Wish they had taken more lessons in counting
before they came over here. During the counting, they must have thought that someone had
escaped, because all the guards were marched up
from the gate and stationed at various places nearer the buildings."

April 6 was a gala day for us, as we received letters from Ethel Prescott, Mildred Elston, and
Chas. Bragin, and that evening there was another
movie. Only black mark against the day was that
I broke out in a bad case of athlete's foot and had
to start daily visits to the clinic for treatment. So
many people have this trouble, and it is not only
uncomfortable but a bother, and I hoped we would
miss it. Our soap supply is so low that to try to
make it last longer, I haven't been soaping myself
thoroughly lately, so I suppose that is how I collected the germ."

In addition to this, for April 6, my notes read
"The very mean Japanese lieutenant who has been
responsible for the recent cuts in our food is said

to have left for other parts; some say to Los Banos with the group that left today, others say to Quezon Institute because he is sick, while others say he has returned to Japan. Hope he doesn't die peacefully before our boys get at him."

April 8 "The morning music woke us at three o'clock and the children wanted to see the large group off to Los Banos, so we went downstairs and saw them all loaded into army trucks. Off they went at about five o'clock. We then had time for another little nap before rising for the day. For the next ten days after this, Ann was in the hospital with measles. This epidemic broke out in January, and one after another, almost all the children came down with it until I thought mine were going to miss it. But no such luck. Two days before Ann was released from the hospital, John broke out and had to go in. My next entry reads:

April 19 "Two letters from Mother today, so my luck continues to hold but I feel sorry for others who know full well their people must be writing them, yet they have never received one letter. The noon meal, which consists only of Lugao (rice cooked with so much water that it is like a soup), corn, or sometimes cold breakfast mush every other day, or one piece of tough, horrible corn bread about two inches square on the alternate days, threatens to be cut out altogether. No soap has been issued us for weeks now, and the little cakes of soap from our Relief Kits are almost gone. I had to waste hours this morning to be registered—some old questions, but on very official looking forms to be sent to Tokyo. The new Commandant harps on this business of bowing and insists we show more respect. We must bow to any and all Japanese and from the waist, and if we are sitting, we must rise and do it properly and this goes for the little children too. Luckily, it doesn't gripe them like it does us, and they think it a big joke and invariably giggle while they are doing it."

April 26. "John is now back in our room but both children look pale and weak. We all had to sign an oath to the Japanese that we would not attempt to escape or to conspire against them. How inane . . . Our internee agents made protest that such a thing could not be binding, but of course the Japanese ignored that with their usual courtesy. Finally, we added an appendage that it was under duress, and they didn't seem to mind at the time but later insisted that we sign it without the appendage 'or else,' so at that tone, what else could we do. One person, an American-born Chinese refused, and they finally put him in jail for the rest of the internment.

We admired his courage, but really signing that document didn't mean a thing to any of us; if any of us had wished to break it, we would have, so he was rather foolish. He was a little peculiar in this regard, we thought, because he insisted that the

Japanese had locked him up, and they should feed and clothe him, and he would not even accept his Red Cross packages or Relief clothing ,and would not even accept things from friends, so the result was that the clothes he wore were finally in shreds, and it puzzled us how on earth he ever got them on and off."

April 29. "Eric and I had our last cup of coffee today and it tasted good."

May 8. "I feel almost too low to write; it seems so useless. Everyone is hungry and there have been more and more cuts at the vegetable market—many days there is nothing to buy. John has had a bad cough for many days, and Ann and I have had intestinal trouble. She has lost two and a half more pounds these past few weeks, and it worries me so. My feet are still bad, and I have to waste hours each morning in a line to be attended to at the clinic. It is such a stubborn trouble, and one foot has to be bandaged and that makes it awkward hobbling about in my bakyas (wooden slip-on clogs). The past few days, in addition to my feet and tummy trouble I have had a bad throat like Quinsey, swollen glands and ear trouble plus fever and not much rest these nights as so many of the children have whooping cough. How I do dream of having some good food and a few luxuries to give my children—it's like a never-ending nightmare—they are so hungry. We really get dizzy from hunger sometimes. I am very tired of washing without soap, and my head never feels clean, but the few slivers I have left must be kept for the children as I must keep them free of athlete's foot, etc. if I possibly can. I refuse to be re-elected for Monitor again, as I feel I have done more than my share and it is time someone else took over the responsibility.

May 12. "Today there was nothing to be had at the market and the food on the line was terrible, but we are still purring over yesterday. It was Eileen Candy's birthday, and there happened to be a number of things available at the vegetable market so we decided to cheer ourselves with a good meal, and this, I must make a note of for future reference. We par-boiled one pound of camotes (sweet potato) then fried our last slice of canned kit bacon, plus native onions (that are so small that it takes half an hour to prepare a handful), added one pound cooked string beans (the local kind that come about a foot long and are tough and tasteless), then added one package of dry soup powder and one bouillon powder, then one of our precious cans of corned beef, added a few spoons of carabao milk and our last tablespoon of cornstarch and simmered the lot. The result was somewhat like a pea soup, and it was delicious. We went to bed feeling almost good. I forgot to add to that recipe that of course we added the camote water and the bean water, but not too much of either because we wanted to have something with some flavour for a change.

May 17. "I made a deal with Dorothy Kephart, who has a supply of good pre-war American soap hoarded up, but who hates to do laundry; for the past four days, in return for enough soap to wash ourselves, I have done her laundry. What a deal and what a wash, but at least we are clean again."

May 30 There is no point in making an entry every day and wasting the paper when we need it so badly for the bathroom. It is really a problem and everyone's old magazines and even library books are meeting a sad end to cope with this need. Eric is in the hospital with enteritis and is very sick indeed, and Ann is in bed with a fever. She and John seem to alternate with their fevers—just hunger and weakness the doctor says, so I just let them rest in bed till they feel strong enough to get up. Terribly tiring for me, visiting the hospital, standing in all lines, doing two laundries, and tending the children. Just to add to things the other day, after the usual 8:30 a.m. roll call, the Japanese ordered another one at 11:30 a.m. just when people were standing in line for their noon spoonful of food. This roll call lasted two and a half hours, so we didn't get the food, then again at 4:30 p.m. so help me if there wasn't another roll call and this wasn't dismissed until 6 p.m. We then stood in line and received our food plus the noon spoonful and was I glad to get to bed that night. The Japanese must feel awfully mean about something."

June 5 "Wonder what I'll build the children up with after this bout. John has had a fever ever since my last entry but snapped out of it today and is so hungry that he wants to eat everything on sight but there is nothing much to give him these days. Our canned goods from the Red Cross kits are almost gone, and of course the children's milk supply ended when I tried to build them up a bit after the measles. I had another few days of inside trouble, terrible cramps and nausea. Wonder will help ever come."

June 18 "The rumors have been good off and on. We hear that Rome has fallen, and a second front has been started, but hunger has depressed us too much to care a great deal; besides, Europe seems so far away from here. I received seven letters from home in one swoop two days ago, and how nice it was to read them all. Eric is sick again with tummy trouble. After having been allowed them for the past couple of months, the daily paper has been discontinued again, so we are unable to check up if any of the rumors are true. The past few weeks, the Japanese have issued just one order after another. First, they wanted a list of all men from fifteen to fifty, and of course this set off another series of rumors as to what they were going to do with them. Next, they want all the men from the gymnasium building to be housed on the third floor of the main building; then they want our men to erect a barbed wire fence atop the outside wall and another bamboo fence covered with sawali to be erected ten meters from the Camp wall. They seem to think that news and food is thrown over to us (and in this they are probably right) but their official announcement is that they don't want the Filipinos to jump over the fence and steal from the internees.

Last week we each received a ration of one small piece of soap, a small bundle of toilet paper, and one kilo of peanuts for each six persons. No supply of oil these days, so we cannot cook anything. No more money anyway . . . great fun."

June 30. "The end of another month, thank goodness, and I wonder just what the next month has in store for us. News has been good but is still too slow for us. So many we knew are passing away—it is really pathetic. Some high official Japanese is to inspect the camp at 10:30 today—'No laundry to show out front,' 'No airing of beds or mattresses,' 'No wearing of housecoats,' 'No preparing of food other than at the main kitchen,' 'Everything to be clean, etc.' and 'Everyone to bow,' . . . Not if I see him first. There is to be a distribution of eggs this afternoon at two pesos each and cassava flour will be available at P19.50 per kilo (that is two pounds between six persons). We cannot buy anything until the July sum is given us, and that will probably be a few more days. Ann was examined yesterday, and like so many others is anemic."

July 16 "There has been nothing worth entering but just have to mention that early this morning there were two big explosions some distance away and perhaps it was oil, because the sky has been black with clouds of smoke all day. This makes us feel a little better because if it is intentional by the Japanese, then that seems a good sign, if it is sabotage, then it shows the Japanese are preoccupied, and if it was accidental, then it is a good loss to them.

Nothing else has happened worth entering, and while our food allowance is less if anything, we seem to have gotten a second wind as far as being hungry is concerned. It doesn't bother us quite as much as it did when things became bad earlier this year, so that is a big help.

There has been plenty of rain but no terrific deluges like last year; even so, we have been confined to the buildings about as much or more, but we don't mind it so much, because the reason is that we are under 'blackout practice' and this, naturally, makes us believe that the Japanese must really be expecting things to happen.

I gave up doing Dorothy Kephart's laundry because it was really an unfair deal, and I am now of the opinion that I should conserve my strength even if we have to go dirty."

July 18. "Yesterday, a couple of Japanese military men came into camp, and we were informed that we all had to be photographed. We were done in groups of five, each displaying a number across his chest. This really made us feel like criminals and there was no smiling 'for the birdie'; we all glared and if looks would kill, that photographer wouldn't have lasted an hour."

In June we had made arrangements to borrow a little more money, and this came through about the middle of July. Then early in August, the Japanese delivered a mean blow by announcing that all money held by internees had to be turned in and it would be put in the Bank of Taiwan for safe keeping. They promised that it would be doled back to us at the rate of P50 per person per month with half that amount for children. This was a big blow to many people because they had borrowed large amounts in case things became worse. It so happened that we didn't have such a large amount to turn in and after it was doled back to us each month, there were just a few hundred pesos left that of course were 'lost' to us.

During August, there always seemed to be reason for being alarmed. First, the Japanese talked a lot about possible air raids and the fact that we should dig ourselves some air raid shelters, but this was impossible owing to the lack of materials as all the Japanese furnished our men with were a few bamboo poles. The fact, too, that it was still the rainy season meant that any holes that were dug would very soon be filled with water. I remember the laugh we had watching the members of the Japanese office staff dig themselves an air raid shelter right near the main building. It was such a miserable looking affair, and after the next good rain it was filled with water.

Some of the people who were living in their shanties did their best to build up some sort of a shelter, but at best, these were very inadequate. Of course we were not particularly 'alarmed' over all this as, actually, we were all looking forward to a bombing like children looking forward to a party; but there were other things to alarm us . . . for instance, they did say that should Manila be bombed, the Japanese would be unable to bring food into the camp and of course, since we were not allowed to contact the outside anymore or to bring any in, it put us in an unpleasant position to even think of. Then, at different intervals, the Japanese would raid one or more rooms and search them thoroughly, and in some cases found internees in possession of more than the PSO allowed. That started another row, and more orders were issued as to what would happen to the next culprit, and an additional few days were given for excess amounts to be turned in.

During this month, our men complained about the food ration and requested that more be allowed us, but none was forthcoming. We also learned that four of our men who had been taken out of camp some time before, had been given long prison sentences to be served in some outside jails. Their crime was that they had smuggled information to the internees as regards war news. We also learned that there would be no more issues of toilet paper (such as it was), as there was none to be had in the Philippines, so I'll leave it to you to figure out how you would have solved this problem. That was a worry that lasted for seven months at least.

Rumors came thick and fast during this month . . . one day we would hear that all the men from eighteen to forty-five years of age were to be sent to Formosa, then again, we would hear that we were all to be sent to Japan, and this didn't help us one bit. In a way, we began to feel sort of numb and just ready for any kind of order they might issue.

A pitiful sight was to see all the aged people being brought in from the various places where they had been allowed to stay for some time. For them to have to pitch in and live the way we were, waiting in lines, etc., was very hard, but of course they couldn't all be hospitalized as there were too many really sick people to be taken care of. I often gave a prayer of thanks that none of the old folk were my relatives; it was bad enough feeling sorry for them and knowing they were someone's relatives, but for them to have been mine would have been very hard. Many of them did not live to see the end, but died off gradually from September on. Early in September we each received a small quantity of corned beef from the camp reserve stock. It amounted to three hundred grams or, one twelve-ounce can for every four internees twice a week, and although that sounds a small amount, it really was a luxury, because we were four, and our can would last two days. We would stir a little in with the morning mush, a little in with the noon lugao, and took the night meal as it came, and believe it or not, we imagined we could feel ourselves getting stronger just to see these specks of meat in our food.

Early in September, we had a practice air alert when about an hour afterwards a supposed real alert sounded. Some were very excited over this, but we were afraid to feel too eager so put it down to their wish to see if we would obey orders. This so-called 'alert' lasted for a few days, so we were allowed to go about our daily business, with restrictions of course. There was another air raid signal the day after, and with this coming on top of a warning by the commandant that all and every small fire must be extinguished during an air raid, the feeling that this was real gradually seeped in, and we felt very excited. Even the fact that our daily rice ration was again cut from four hundred to three hundred grams couldn't dampen our enthusiasm. The reason given for the cut was that they were unable to transport rice about the city on account of the air raid alert. The next buzz of excitement was caused by the fact that dysentery, typhus, and typhoid were said to be reaching epidemic proportions in the city of Manila, and we all had to line up again for another set of injections. Many people, being so weak from lack of food became quite sick after these injections. Ann and John had slight temperatures and had to stay in bed a couple of days, but that was all. Eric and I were not bothered by them. One evening, the musical department (perhaps feeling happy over the recent air alerts) played some patriotic numbers during the musical program and contrary to orders, many people applauded. This apparently irked the Japanese to no end because right away, they insisted that the programs be discontinued and then, to make matters worse, they cut our rice down another fifty grams. But a few days later, after our men talked and tried to reason, the fifty grams were restored to us. September 21 finally arrived and this important day I must try to describe to you in detail. It was the first day the Americans bombed Manila and one of the most exciting in our lives.

I had my laundry finished and out before breakfast as usual, in case of being confined to the room, and by nine that morning, with my chores done, I was sitting out in front with Eric, whose duty was also over for the day (he used to get up at 3:30 a.m. to cook). The children had gone to the Playhouse at the rear of the building. We noticed that there were many Japanese planes up, and they seemed to be engaged in mock warfare which we watched with little interest. Then, out of the blue, and it was a perfect day too, came this wonderful formation of silver-looking planes, big and very high powered by the sound of them. Gunfire started and some Japanese planes dropped. There was a yell of, "they're ours! They're Americans up there!" and we stood and watched open-mouthed. The actions were perfect; the formation broke, some going in pursuit of the Japanese planes which were becoming conspicuous by their absence, while most of them dive-bombed to their objectives. And then the noise and fun really started. Everything seemed to be happening at once. The Japanese officials rushed out of their office and ordered us all into the building but Eric and I were already on our way through to get the children. By this time, the Japanese anti-aircraft had gotten into action and shells were bursting and shrapnel was falling as we ran from the back door. We met the children about halfway as they were making for the building, and grabbing one each, we made quick time back to the building. What excitement there was. People were crying and laughing and we all kept repeating "isn't it wonderful." We were told over the radio that anyone caught outside or looking out of a window would be shot and armed Guards were placed everywhere, even in the tower, but we had to see more and did. The noise of the planes and of the explosions was still terrific, and we found that by crouching down on the hall floor against the room wall, we were out of sight of the guards on the tower, yet could see up through the patio windows, and we had a wonderful view of the American planes. We saw each one as they dived to bomb, and just before they were out of sight, we were lucky enough to see the bombs leave the plane and drop down and then boom. This kept up for hours. Wave after wave of planes would come and bomb and smoke poured up from everywhere we looked. What a mess things must have been, and what a noise there was. No one was scared—not even the children; we were all too excited. We knew that the Americans knew we were there and that any hit on the building would be accidental.

All power was turned off and as fires were not allowed, there was no cooking but who cared. The water failed and the emergency tanks on top of the building had to be used but only for the most essential things. During a lull early in the afternoon we were doled out two emergency biscuits apiece but these did very little toward filling us up. They were a small hard biscuit made of rice flour, a little salt, soda, and vinegar, very little shortening, and water to mix. They were cut out with a top off a corned beef can, so were about two-and-a-half by one-and-a-half inches in size. The air raid was over in time for an evening meal to be prepared, and after the exciting day we had, the food didn't seem to taste half as bad as the day before. Many people who had supplies of canned goods on hand fixed themselves a wonderful spread to celebrate the day. Rumors were flying before evening about the amount of damage that had been done, and if they were true, then the waterfront was really ruined. Ships were sunk in the harbor, planes were caught on the ground in large numbers, and ammunition and oil dumps had been fired. It all sounded wonderful, and we went to bed feeling very light of heart.

Perhaps I have mentioned it before, but in case not, I will repeat that each morning "wake up" music was played from the music room and this would consist of two or three numbers that sounded over all loud speakers and reached every part of the camp and grounds, and on the morning after the bombing the selections were "I Cover the Waterfront," "Pennies from Heaven," and "It Looks Like Rain in Cherry Blossom Lane." When we caught the significance in the titles, we all went about with large smiles on our faces.

Breakfast had no sooner been served on the morning of the 22—in fact, I don't think they were through—when another air raid alarm sounded and the fun was on for the second day. When I say "fun" I should add that while it was fun to us to know that the enemy was getting what they deserved, it was also fun because it meant the end was in sight. We did not lose sight of the fact that the whole thing was terrible, because we knew while all this went on, good American lives were being lost, and in and around Manila, loyal Filipinos and other nationalities were losing their lives either from being too close to objectives, or from the shrapnel that was falling everywhere. I heard there was just one injury received from falling shrapnel in the camp and this was not fatal. During the second day of bombing, the planes continued to come over in waves, and as quite a large piece of shrapnel had come in the window of the next room to us, we decided we had better take what precaution we could, so most of us took to the floor and in this, I felt fortunate, because at the head of Ann and John's beds was a solid-looking supporting column, so I pushed their beds apart a little and put a grass mat and bedding on the concrete floor and there we sat huddled behind the pillar and when things sounded particularly close and thick, I would pull the beds together over our heads and we would lie there and I would tell the children stories, or we might play guessing games or anything to pass the time.

There were several alarms during the next few days, but the action must have been elsewhere because planes didn't appear over Manila. We were reduced to a definite two-meal-a-day schedule, and this meant such a long stretch in between that we would take a few spoons of mush from our plates in the mornings and save them to eat around noon. But that didn't help much, and the children would be fretful and hungry before supper time. For a while they were able to serve the children only—a small portion of rice and one fourth of a cup of carabao milk at noon—but this didn't last. By the end of September, we were still under a partial blackout but were permitted to sit outside for a while in the evenings in the semi dark. Early in October, the monthly allowance of PSO was reduced to P25, as the vegetable market had been done away with and very little was available through the canteen. There was no need of much money.

After the first week in October, they began serving three meals a day again, but still on the old basis of leftover breakfast mush with a little vegetable green or doubtful gravy added, but at least it was hot—if watery—and seemed like a meal.

A little later on, the camp's ducks had to be killed as there was not even enough garbage to keep them alive any longer. "Duck soup" written on the menu board was the cause of much excitement, and while you couldn't really put your finger on the flavor on account of the small number of ducks per internee, nevertheless, the soup seemed to have a little body to it that added greatly to the meal.

During the same week, all the front grounds were declared out of bounds to internees, and truck loads of Japanese soldiers came in and took up residence in hastily erected tents. Large quantities of materials, crates, mysterious looking packages, and pieces of machinery were brought in and piled high in rows all over the front grounds. We wondered much about all this and were just afraid that the next thing they might do would be to erect anti-aircraft guns, but this never came to pass.

Since most of the remaining grounds were taken up with vegetable gardens and shanties, that left nowhere to walk but around the main building; however, with the diet we were on, we felt in little need of exercise. Anyone caught looking at the articles or being found on the front grounds was to be punished.

During these few weeks when the American planes did not appear again over Manila, the musical department sometimes started the day with "Lover Come Back to Me" and to mention a few other times when their humor made us smile, after we had to turn over our money, they played "I Can't Give You Anything but Love," "I Got Plenty O' Nuttin'," and "Never Felt Better, Never Had Less," and once, when rumor had it that an attempt had been made to kill Hitler, the next day's music was "Ding-Dong! The Witch Is Dead."

On October 15, after what had seemed such a long wait, there was another air raid and we saw planes overhead once more. Not that we expected there to be anything left to bomb after the terrific pounding they gave it in September, but with the planes coming, it seemed as though help for us was closer—in fact, many of us were overly optimistic and expected the U.S. Fleet to enter the Manila Bay any day. We spent many hours during the dark evenings discussing how we thought we would be released, and we would become so excited with anticipation that it was hard to talk. After the raid on the fifteenth of October, the commandant and his staff decided to take up residence on the ground floor of the education building rather than in the small one-story place they had occupied. No doubt they felt they would be safer in a larger building, though it did happen before the end that the larger place was shelled while the small one went unscratched. Our men had to move out of the education building and find places elsewhere.

There were air raids and air alerts daily for almost that whole week, and we wondered afterwards if the concentrated effort might not have been a cover-up for the landing at Leyte. We grew very tired of being cooped up in our room for hour after hour. Though it didn't seem so bad when there was action overhead, more often during the week, the planes were some distance away but we had to stay in our rooms until the "all clear" sounded. One needed a vast amount of patience to keep the children amused and good. If I remember, Joan Hunter's birthday was on one of these days because I remember going outdoors early with my dish pan to gather fresh hibiscus, and I just managed to fill my pan before the raids started for the day. I spent the next hour making a lovely long red hibiscus lei and this kept the children amused. I had enough blossoms left over to make Ann a small one, and she was quite thrilled about it. I finished the one for Joan with a nice ribbon bow and as John, her husband, was on guard duty at the back door, I gave it to him to take to her at the first opportunity.

When General MacArthur landed on Leyte, the news reached the camp via the grapevine in quick time, or so I thought, but I have since learned that it must have been received on the secret radio the men had in camp. Many of us had heard the rumor by nightfall but were still doubtful of it when Don Bell, the camp announcer, came on the air to make the daily announcements. He spoke of the rice that the Japanese were late in bringing into camp as having at last arrived, then after a pause he added, "Well, better Leyte than never." That was a very clever pun, and quite a little murmur ran through the listening crowd. Word was soon carried to those who hadn't heard it, but it must have been lost on the Japanese because that was the last we heard of the matter.

November started with the commandant trying again to impress his will upon us regarding bowing and showing respect. He stated that henceforth, at roll call both morning and evening, we must bow low from the waist to which ever official came by. We treated this as we had done before, and many of us refused to bow, so adopting the attitude that we would have to learn, he had all monitors and supervisors take lessons from his lieutenant for part of three days in a row. These people, in turn, had to show the other internees the correct method, and we were supposed to practice it until we had it perfect. It was tempting to continue to be obstinate about it, but since it turned out that the monitors would be held responsible if we failed, we finally gave in, so twice a day saw all of us, even down to children smaller than Ann and John, bowing from the waist. Days on end, that nasty lieutenant would come around and stand there while we bowed. We were not allowed to return to a standing position until he felt good and ready to move on to the next group. For some reason, that seemed to be the thing that made me really mad; it always took an effort to bow. I used to think, "we'll do it now, but boy oh boy, just wait a while, and with a bit of luck the positions may be reversed." There was another air raid on November 5, and during this one, three men were arrested for looking at our planes. They were taken to the front guard house and made to stand looking at the hot sun until late that day. There was another alarm early the next day and during this, we had a very unpleasant experience when a large number of guards with fixed bayonets, plus some officials, suddenly closed off the main building. A guard was stationed at every corner and every staircase, and as we had no warning as to what all this was for, we began to feel very jittery. We had often discussed the possibility that the Japanese might try to kill all of us before the end, and at this time, for some reason, we began to talk of it in whispers and we realized how easily they could accomplish such a thing. We were careful not to let the children hear us, but I for one began to feel very limp inside and started to think sort of desperately of any way out of it should such a thing take place either now or at a later date. All my thoughts ended in a blank wall. We were prisoners, and there was no way out. If they chose to shoot us or kill us in any other way, we would be powerless to stop them, and the thought of such a dreadful end for Ann and John and all the other kiddies was too terrible to think of, and I would have to force myself to think of something more cheerful. Perhaps that sounds pessimistic, but remember, we had heard rumors that it was supposedly a fact that the Japanese intended to kill us rather than let the Americans free us. We understand now that they did have that intention, but events crept up on them unexpectedly at the end, and they were too worried about their own hides. To return to the event I was discussing, after what seemed an endless wait, the group arrived at our room. But by this time, of course, we knew it must be just another search because we had heard no other noise. And search they did; they opened everything—searched through luggage, looked under beds—everywhere. Luckily, there were many patched mattresses at this date, so my penciled notes remained safe inside Ann's mattress. I had made many patches on it so that one would not be obvious and had chosen her mattress because it was reasonably thick, and my papers were sewn in, then taken out, on many occasions. At last, they decided they weren't interested in anything in our room so passed on to the next, and we all sat down and breathed a sigh of relief.A little before this date, I forgot to mention that at bedtime one night, Ann was fooling in her bed, and she toppled over the end and landed head-first on the concrete floor with such a terrific noise that it sounded just like a crack. I held her for a while but couldn't tell whether she was just sleepy or perhaps going unconscious, so I took her to the doctor and he kept her under observation for a few hours and said it apparently was a slight concussion. He told me what to do, so I carried her back to bed, and though it was too dark to see her—and of course we weren't allowed a light—I sat on one of the children's tiny folding stools right beside her bed all night and listened to her breathing as the doctor said to keep a close watch for any change. She mumbled quite a lot during the night but didn't seem to get any worse. I had her in bed for a few days and she seemed sort of dopey, but it passed and she brightened and was able to get up.

During the rest of November, there were air raids off and on and these helped to cheer us. The internees were becoming thinner and thinner, and many were dying from beriberi. Other than wondering how long it was going to be, all we could think of was food; we had, perhaps, gone slightly crazy about it, but the fact remains that we would sit and discuss food by the hour. We would plan full menus of what we were going to eat if we ever got out of it alive, and stupid now though it sounds, many of us were using precious paper to copy recipes down. I used to see old people and little children just able to write, all writing recipes, and in this, I was just as bad as the rest. Though at the time, I did think I was only copying recipes that sounded different, while others were jotting down anything at all just so long as it pertained to food. In front of the children, we tried not to talk about it. We explained to them that this was just how things were, and that if we talked of it, we might feel worse. In this, Ann was just perfect. She tried very hard not to talk of it, but of course poor John was smaller, and he used to ask always for something to eat.

Before the end of this month, we had to face the fact that Eric had beriberi. His ankles were very swollen, so we were at least thankful that he had the outward type. I don't know the correct names, but we used to speak of beriberi as being either the outward or inward type, and with the latter, it was worse, because you never knew how bad you were. With the other, you knew you had to swell a good deal before it was too late, so you can imagine, we used to measure Eric's ankles practically daily. He felt listless and weak and had lost such a lot of weight, so although he didn't feel bad enough to take up another bed in the hospital, he did quit work, and other than a few days spent working in the vegetable garden, he did not work again before the end; however, he didn't feel badly about this because he had worked all through the three years, right from the beginning when, at that time, there were many able-bodied men who did nothing but sit or play cards, refusing any kind of camp labor.

The early part of December was just a long nightmare of hungry days and nights, of friends dying, and children complaining, of dark nights—even darker than before—because even when there wasn't an air raid, all hall and room lights had to be out with the exception of a small-shaded lamp at each corner of the halls. When there was a raid, even this was out, and to go to the bathroom, it was necessary to walk with your hands out in front like a sleep walker to ward off anyone else. Everything was done by feel and it is wonderful how correct you become at finding things in the dark. About December 15, there was much talk about whether we would receive relief kits again at Christmas. We tried hard not to think of them or to expect them, knowing so well that the Japanese were probably too busy and too mad to let us have them even if they had been shipped over. However, the rumor persisted for weeks until well after New Year, when we just had to forget about them, but it was hard. About the middle of December there were more air raids, and we used to think, "Surely they have bombed everything there is to be bombed. How long now?"

In the early days when a person passed away, the next of kin was allowed out on a pass to arrange the burial and a proper hearse would come into the camp hospital for the body. But 1944 was quite different, and no one was allowed out to make any arrangements. A Filipino with a broken down caratela and a very bony little horse would come in with a long empty box of the poorest type of wood. In full sight of all of us, he would lead his horse out again with the box, its burden jostling along, one end sticking out of the back of the caratela. And in this undignified way, a person left the company of his fellow men. By the end of 1944, this fellow had to come and go constantly to take care of the dead, and don't think that there was any proper burial for these poor unfortunates. They were just dumped into a hole anywhere, and relatives of those who passed away during those months will probably never know where their loved ones are resting. I might add that the same box was reused all the time.

The Japanese became obsessed with the idea that if we wanted more food, we must grow it, and they kept insisting that we make more gardens, plant more vegetables, and that more men should be doing this work. They were too stubborn to listen to our arguments against it. They even went so far as to bribe those who did garden work with the ability to purchase cigarettes, tobacco, and sometimes, rice. And these supplies were withheld from distribution to all regardless of what type of work the other people did. Our men really didn't have the strength to do hours of hard digging under the hot sun in the condition they were in, and the vegetables gained—if they ever did grow, and many did not on account of lack of water—would not be of sufficient value to compensate for the energy used in growing and harvesting them.

We were on a starvation diet now. The meals consisted mostly of breakfast—one small ladle of watery mush and 1 cup of weak tea, coffee, or perhaps just hot water; lunch—one small ladle of watery vegetable stock or perhaps none at all; and dinner—one small ladle of watery rice, sometimes corn, or perhaps camotes, with one ladle of watery gravy, and don't forget, we had been leading up to this starvation period with inadequate meals for at least that full year. Many times, we would be sixteen hours without anything to eat, and many people would faint from weakness. In the showers, you could see the terrible effect on the people; their skin would hang in folds and their seats were vanishing altogether. I had a routine of gently patting the children on the bottom to get them to go to sleep at nights, and by December, I had to admit that there was very little left under the skin but bone. It was a dreadful feeling to see your own children just fading away before your eyes, and yet there was nothing we could do. We had been in the habit of giving Ann and John an extra spoon of our food, but one of the doctors pointed out that if it came to the point of us all starving to death, the adults would go first, so it was best not to give the children any of our food unless we wanted them to live on alone. So, hard as it was, we had to refuse them any from our plates. The cereal ration was cut down twice during the latter part of December until we were receiving 161 grams per day, but the meals tasted better because during a few weeks at this time, there was a supply of soy meal added to the night meal and this made it thicker and better, and very often we had camotes in addition, which made those days seem festive. A rather amusing note should be made here as regards the extras we received with the Christmas meal. It seemed there was a certain amount of jam and chocolate on hand, and it was decided to give this to the internees as a treat for Christmas. Well, there were more notices, meetings, and discussions about these two items than you can imagine. Finally, it was put to a vote that we should decide to have either: the jam served on Christmas eve at the canteen on the basis of one two-pound tin for three canteen cards (eighteen people), or that we should mix the jam with a number of green papayas from the camp gardens, cook the two, and serve them on the morning mush. A similar idea for the chocolate was to either: serve it at the canteen at nine 30-gram rolls of chocolate per three canteen cards (eighteen people), or mix it with the noon meal and serve chocolate lugao for lunch. Well, you see by this time, everyone was scared to lose the tiniest particle of food that should rightly be theirs, so they were afraid that once those items were put in the kitchen to be handled in bulk, a finger would dip in here and there and so precious grams would be lost, so the voting resulted in: 2,700 for direct issue through the canteen cards with just 280 voting for it to be served through the kitchen. When all the waiting in line was done, and the jam and chocolate had been divided between the groups of eighteen people, the result was one and one-quarter tablespoons of jam per person, and half a piece of chocolate per person. A full piece of chocolate measured one and one-eighth inches in diameter, by three-quarters of an inch thick. I can remember the children just taking licks off their chocolate to make it last, and the jam we ate slowly off a spoon so as not to lose the flavor by putting it in any of our food. The main Christmas menu for the day, by the way, was as follows: breakfast—one ladle of mush with sweetened chocolate and cocomilk. (I don't know where they got the extra chocolate from; they had a little sugar on hand; and cocoa-nuts came in the day before, so the men were able to make the cocomilk.) Lunch—one ladle vegetable stock thickened with soy bean meal. Dinner—fried rice with tiny shreds of canned meat and a double serving of camotes and rice. This was indeed a banquet, and we saved a small portion each to enjoy before the children went to bed.

I have left out an important thing that happened two days before Christmas, and that was that another search took place by Japanese MP's and soldiers, and at the end, a Mr. E. E. Johnson was arrested and taken out of camp. Then, of all unheard-of things, they arrested Mr. Grinnell, chairman of the Committee, Mr. Duggleby, and a Mr. C. L. Larsen. These three men were placed in the camp jail without any explanation as to why, and this had us all worried. These men had worked so hard for the camp and had done a wonderful job in carrying out the Japanese orders to the internees, yet here they were being put in jail. Aside from the extra food we received, there was no reason to feel pleased about Christmas 1944. Eric did receive five cigars and four cigarettes, and they helped him. There were some games for the children in the playhouse, and each child received a small piece of coconut candy.

While we waited in line for the evening meal that day, the person behind me pushed a piece of paper into my hand and said "Read that and pass it back." It read "The Commander-in Chief, the

Officers, and the men of the American Forces of Liberation in the Pacific wish their gallant allies, the People of the Philippines, all the blessings of Christmas and the realization of their fervent hopes for the New Year. Christmas 1944." I passed it back and the person said that it was one of many that had been dropped from planes that day. This message was whispered about camp until all knew of it. Two days later, another search was made of the rooms on our floor and the result was that a copy of that message was found on a woman two rooms away. She was given a severe talking to and instructions were issued right away that any leaflets dropped from any planes should be turned in to the Japanese office immediately. Anyone found typing copies of same and giving it any publicity would be severely dealt with. Another paper was found on a person the day after that, and she was confined to her quarters for seven days. The day before New Year 1945, the children were playing out in front of the main building for just a short while, and Johnny was digging holes with an old rusty can opener he had found. He must have been in a squatting position, and when he bumped the can opener against a stone, it jerked up and the point scratched his eye. There was just the tiniest mark visible, and I almost didn't take him to the doctor, but he complained and kept rubbing it so I took him to Dr. Bloom. To my surprise, he said it would be necessary to operate. January 1 was the beginning of a worrying month for me, and a very uncomfortable one for poor John. He had been given a sedative while still in the children's hospital in the main building, then carried to the main hospital a little after nine that morning, and while Dr. Bloom was operating, there was another air raid. The doctor said the operation was a success, but that in the child's weakened condition, he might be slow to heal. We would go visit him every afternoon, and the poor kiddie was in such pain that he had to have injections of medicine to deaden it. After a couple of days, there was no change, so Dr. Bloom ordered a fever treatment for him. I had never heard of this, but the doctor explained to me that when the body is in a fever, it promotes healing in the eye, so poor John had to be given typhoid shots daily, but this didn't help either. Finally, the doctor decided to operate again as the infection had spread a little and this was to be done on January 6. He was drugged already with a sedative when planes came over and more bombing started, so the doctor postponed it, but he said it would have to be done the following day regardless. He had to be given another sedative, and then again the bombers came, but this time, the hospital orderly (Dr. Fletcher's son) carried Johnny over, and Dr. Bloom operated once more and they continued to keep him in a fever. After more anxious days, the doctor announced that it was beginning to heal, and my, did we feel thankful. John was in the hospital for the rest of January, and we did our best to take him little extras when we could. He became so very hungry that when we would visit him, the first thing he would ask was "do you have anything for me to eat" until it used to make me want to cry. Even Ann used to save him some of her food, and a friend of ours named Tommy Chapman, who had a little vegetable garden by his shanty, used to give me a lettuce as often as he could. This, we would separate and wash well, and John would sit up and nibble happily on it like a rabbit. At this time, we knew of no source where we could borrow any money like the year before, but we did know that there was a Japanese guard on the wall who was being bribed to allow certain amounts of rice and sugar in, and people were paying high prices for even the smallest amounts. We talked about the possibility of getting some because we really felt desperate about Johnny. He had lost so much more weight and looked so thin and pale that we doubted if he would live long. The only money acceptable to the party outside the wall for rice was good Filipino or American currency, and as we hadn't either, Tommy Chapman came to our rescue and gave us some for an IOU in American dollars. The amount of rice we finally received was a very miserable amount, but by dividing it carefully, we managed to cook a little each day until the end of January, and of this, we gave Ann a little each day too. Eric was in a very weak condition by now, with his ankles and legs so swollen that he could barely manage to hobble about in his bakyas. He had great difficulty in making the stairs even once a day, so it fell to me to stand in all lines and do all chores, and I was thankful that I was strong enough to do it. I had dropped to ninety pounds which was not bad in comparison, and aside from a marked tiredness when I was climbing the stairs, I didn't feel bad at all and I hadn't any signs of beriberi.

Rumors were strong throughout January and bombings were frequent—in fact, during this month, our planes would come over and the downtown signal would not even sound and several times there was no anti-aircraft fire at all. I remember the evening the Japanese began burning their records. From our window, we could look right into the yard behind the commandant's old office, and the Japanese soldiers spent hours burning piles and piles of papers. One day we would hear that the commandant and his staff intended on leaving the camp, then the next day, he would change his mind or perhaps have it changed for him. We heard several explosions at different times and saw many fires throughout Manila and surrounding districts, so it seemed clear that the Japanese were busy demolishing, and that the Americans had truly landed on the island of Luzon, though that sounded too good to be true after all this waiting. Just the same, excitement ran high because there was so much action going on in and around

Manila, and the Japanese seemed so agitated that we just knew things must be coming to a head. I remember the day when the Japanese killed a carabao and took much time in cutting it into tiny strips and drying it in the sun, and they had their things all packed and parked out in front near the roadway, so it did look as though they expected to have to make their exit at any time. Toward the end of the month, the commandant made a fuss because the doctors were putting starvation and malnutrition as the causes of death on several death certificates. He said this was an insult to the Japanese and he ordered them to be changed, but Dr. Stevenson refused so he was put in jail.

Just before the end of the month, John was able to leave the hospital, but he still had a bandage over his eye and even after that was removed, we still had to keep him quiet and not let him look at the light.

At this date, Ann was looking very pale and thin but kept cheerful and was so understanding about the lack of food, that although she was always terribly hungry, she did her best not to talk about it.

On February 1 and 2, the explosions around Manila seemed almost continuous, and fires were visible on all sides of the camp. The Japanese seemed to be making another start to leave because they loaded trucks with almost all the food they could find, and much of it was rightly ours. They took everything ready for picking from the gardens—fruits and vegetables alike—and what seemed worse, they took much of our supply of precious rice. It did look as though they expected to take to the hills for some time; however, even with all this preparation, the commandant and his staff, plus rather a large number of Japanese soldiers, still remained—waiting for the official word to leave, no doubt.

Looking back later, this should have been evidence enough that our men were near, but we had learned through long years that things don't happen as fast as you hope, so, after much talk as to the possibility of obtaining more rice for Ann and John, Eric and I decided that we may even have two weeks more to wait, and that if we could get extra rice to last that long, it would be wise to do so. I made enquiries to see what I could get for my diamond ring, as we had heard that jewelry was being accepted in lieu of money, and I must add here that in the first of this letter, when I described how the Japanese came to our home, I left out one thing, because at the time, it seemed to be making the description too long, but now I must explain that when the Japanese demanded our jewelry, I noticed that Louise Craven turned the stone of her engagement ring to the inside of her hand and then she did her best to keep that hand out of the Japanese view, so I thought if she was going to take a chance, I may as well too. I did the same, and neither of us gave up our wedding or engagement rings. I kept mine all the internment until this time in early February. Just to tell you how they were bleeding the internees, the best offer I could get was two kilos of raw rice—imagine that. Well we talked it over some more and decided that the ring was useless as it was, and even the smallest amount of rice was better than none, and if we cooked one hundred grams each day, the two kilos would last the two weeks, so just before noon on February 3, I gave up my ring and was told that it would probably take until noon the next day to make the contacts and get the rice in. If I had only known...

Right after lunch that day, I did a little washing and as I hung my clothes on the line, three planes roared overhead very low, and I looked up expecting to see the usual 'fried egg' (rising sun insignia), but to my amazement, there were the stars and stripes and not a shot was being fired. I had seen plenty of our planes by this date, but none close enough to really identify the insignia, and it is hard to describe what a thrill it was. Everyone within sight was looking up and cheering, and I dashed up to my room and said to the others "Did you see them?" Some had, and some had missed them and were almost tearful over it. We talked about how wonderful it was, and when the children woke from their siesta, they were so upset that they hadn't been awake to see the planes. A little after that, word went around camp that the pilot of one of the planes had dropped his goggles with a note attached that read "Roll out the barrel; Christmas is coming tomorrow or the day after." Everyone was terribly excited, but I was so afraid to believe it that I even tried to contact the person who had picked up the goggles. Perhaps he was afraid of being questioned by the Japanese, so refused to admit he was the one; however, my search drew a blank. Just to talk of it though, gave us a lift, whether true or not.

That evening, I had just put the children to bed when I heard that people looking from some of the windows could see flares and hear tanks and shooting and almost right away, some Japanese guards came to those rooms with fixed bayonets and ordered all people away from the windows. Anyone caught looking out was to be shot. Most people seemed so keyed up and excited that I remember I was deliberately pessimistic. It seemed too big a thing to get excited over and then perhaps be let down, so I got the children off to sleep after telling them that daddy and I thought it was probably some Filipino guerillas starting some trouble for the Japanese. And after that, I got ready for bed too, thinking that if it wasn't, I would not be one of those who had wasted precious strength by staying up all night for nothing. Well, I hadn't been in bed long when word came along that there was shooting at the front gate, so I thought, "If this is for bad or good, I'd better be dressed at least," so

I got up, but at that moment a roar almost like one huge voice sounded through the main building—just two words at first—They're here!

People were racing madly through the halls yelling it. "Yes, the Americans, out front, no fooling," and as people zipped from their rooms to the front stairs, it was just a mad scramble. Last I had seen of Eric was when he left us to go to bed in his room on the third floor, but I didn't wait to find out if he was still there. I had to see for myself, and right then, so I threw on a housecoat and got the children up and in wraps, and then I rushed them to the front stairs. But halfway down was as far as we could go, and from there all I could see was a sea of heads clear to the front door. I said to the children "this won't do, let's go down the back stairs," so we rushed down the long hall and down the back stairs to the back door and there, we bumped into Tommy Chapman. He had lost his wife and child in the crowd so kindly helped me with the children, and there, right in the roadway a few yards from the doorway was a huge American tank. What a beautiful sight that was, and one I'll never forget. A few soldiers were standing by it, and they were looking in wonderment at the crowd of people. Perhaps they wondered if we were all demented and indeed, we must have looked it—ragged and thin, sort of dazed with wonder that the thing we had waited so long for had really come to pass. People were crawling over the tank, patting and kissing it, and others were crying and laughing together. I did my share of the latter, and just couldn't help it. Tommy lifted first John then Ann up to touch the tank, and the children were just bewildered by it all, but I still think their idea of an American soldier would be best described as a big strong superman type who killed Japanese with one hand and gave them food with the other. I remember how sad they seemed when I had to explain that the food was, perhaps, not unpacked yet, or that it was still on the way, and that they would have to be patient until at least the next day. It was still impossible to get to the front of the building, but we had seen an American tank and American soldiers, and that was sufficient, so I took the children back upstairs where we met Eric, who had apparently done much the same as we had but we had missed him in the crowd.

People began opening food that they had been keeping for worse days, and since we had nothing to celebrate with, another person who had a supply of rice let us have some, and I remember, late as it was, Eric went down to the patio and lit up his charcoal stove, and put the rice on to cook in a five-pound Lactogen! milk-formula can, and when it was done, the can was nearly full, and the rice was nicely cooked—not all watery the way we had been having it. The children were wide awake and wouldn't have missed it for the world, so it must have been well after eleven o'clock when we sat down to a plate of boiled rice each, and did it taste good! We shared it with a few of the others from my room who hadn't any, and everyone was very happy. I finally got Ann and John off to sleep, and they were really exhausted. Eric and I sat for some time longer in the hall, discussing with various others the latest developments, and we heard then about the trouble in the education building, but before I mention it, I had better tell things in the order of their happening.

It seems that when the tanks smashed their way through the front gates, the soldiers didn't quite know what to expect from the quietness of the darkened building, and they had their guns ready. As the tanks rumbled up the driveway, men on the leading tank are said to have called out "Are you Americans in there?" and when our people, peering from the darkened windows, realized who it was, they answered "Yes!" and so on. Crowds gathered in the lobby to rush out, but some of our men had the sense to keep them in because just then, Lt. Abiko walked out front and was about to hurl a hand grenade, so a soldier on the leading tank shot him. Then, it seems, the commandant and a few of the civilian Japanese walked out and gave themselves up, and they were duly thrown into the jail that our people had just broken into to release Dr. Stevenson and the others.

After hearing from our people that the rest of the Japanese were housed in the education building, some of the tanks rumbled over there and the soldiers were anxious to shoot or capture, as necessary, the rest of the Japanese. But they were a few paces ahead and had barricaded themselves in the building, at the same time, holding as hostages some two hundred internees who lived on other floors. The Japanese threatened to shoot them if the Americans attempted to come and get them, and they were heavily armed enough to have carried out their threat. So that night passed by with those in our building celebrating and being so happy, while just a stone's throw away, our fellow internees were putting in an uncomfortable and nervous night. All Sunday, the interpreters dickered back and forth, and twice, the Americans, after calling out to the internees to keep down on the floor in one spot, opened fire and just riddled one side of the building. The Japanese inside rushed to the floor where our people were and, I understand, some of them even tried to crawl underneath them to hide.

Finally, a bargain was made, and on Monday morning the Japanese all filed out with their side-arms. They were safely escorted to the city limits and there allowed to go, but of course, there was no need to fret over that, as I'm sure the grapevine worked rapidly and those who were not killed by Filipinos were soon captured.

To return to Sunday for us . . . extra rice was cooked, so although the food was still tasteless, at least we had enoughof it. Supplies of extra rice, soybean meal, and corn were brought in from the seminary and we had all we could eat. When not eating, sitting, or talking about our good fortune, we would take little walks and watch the soldiers setting up guns and being generally busy. These men seemed so sorry to see so many hungry people—and especially children—that they gave away their rations of vitamin chocolate and gum and even their food until some were standing in our lines and eating rice and corn.

Our two kilos of rice finally arrived, and as the party who had given us some on the night of February 3 didn't want it returned and we were getting enough to eat, there it sat. In a day or so when the Filipinos were allowed to enter camp, I gave the two kilos to a fellow who used to be a beauty operator at a place near the Elk's Club that I used to patronize before the war. He, like many others, came into camp, and for services rendered, received leftover food from the internees. They were very grateful, as the food situation on the outside was very acute. Well, so much for the fate of my engagement ring, but that was just unfortunate.

Fires and explosions continued in Manila. Word soon came in that the Japanese were burning and killing as they retreated, and no one in the city or suburbs was safe. We could see the flames from the camp, and the sky was one huge red glow. It all seemed so wicked and cruel, yet there was nothing that could be done. The eight hundred men who had fought their way down from the north just to reach Santo Tomas before we all came to a sad end, had orders to take Santo Tomas and hold it. The forces in the rear were still on their way, so there wasn't much the eight hundred could have done had they been allowed to follow the Japanese into the city. Besides, the Japanese had doubtlessly made plans some time before to ruin the city before they gave up or left it, so no matter how many Americans had been after them, I'm afraid Manila was doomed from the first.

On Tuesday, February 6 American military men were in full charge of the camp and then we began to realize how swell it was not to see Japanese at every turn—no more bowing and no more roll calls—we were free at last. There was no rushing outside the gates as we had pictured, for the simple reason that the enemy was still everywhere; the main army of Japanese had retreated across the river to the city, but small bands and stray snipers were left behind, and they still caused trouble on our side of the river—and especially to us when they would shoot into the grounds. Santo Tomas was the front line for about a week, and for a few days it was really isolated. On February 8, when the Japanese began shelling the camp from across the river, we hardly dared to think what would happen if the forces were long in coming from the north and the Japanese decided to come back; the fate we would all meet was all too clear, and I, for one, had to force myself to think of more cheerful things.

When the first shells hit the building, they tore huge holes in one of the corner rooms that was occupied mostly by older women. I was fortunate in the fact that our room was on the opposite side of the building, and although large pieces of flying metal and concrete hit around and near our room, piercing holes in the hallway walls during later hits, our room was actually never touched. We would have been safe had we stayed there, but everyone became rather frightened and excited, and while we were warned not to go outside, we still seemed to think we should be near an entrance in case greater damage occurred to the building; in fact, word even went around that it was possible the Japanese might use planes to bomb the whole camp and be done with it. Looking back now, I don't think they had a plane left to do such a job; however, all the people flocked as near to the rear door as possible, because the front one was too good a target, and here, they jammed themselves up tight.

No one seemed to know just who had been killed and who had been injured during that first shelling, but after a while, word went around, and when we heard the names of the victims, it filled us with such sorrow and dread that any joy of being free seemed to vanish. We never knew where the next shell might hit but lived in the hope that they would come from just the one direction. In this, we were lucky. The first night of shelling was a nightmare that I would not like to have to go through again. Just like so many sheep, we joined the rush to be near the rear entrance and found some space behind the food-serving counter. Eric's presence of mind to bring the children's folding stools along helped us out for several hours, as we were able to sit and hold the children. But as the night progressed and they couldn't sleep comfortably in such a cramped condition, we put them up on a shelf that was used by the food servers for their personal items such as cups, plates, and spoons. This was about eighteen inches wide and by lying on their sides, the children were at least able to stretch out. Eric stood by one while I stood by the other to see that they didn't fall off, and when they became restless, we would turn them over. When small children are tired, even the noise of shells and gunfire isn't enough to keep them awake, and Ann and John slept fairly well though, naturally, they felt stiff the next day. Around us, hundreds of others sat or stood, but I don't think anyone managed to sleep. Shells were bursting all around and every so often one would hit the building, but by then, all the rooms on that side of the building had been vacated. Two big rooms on the ground floor had hurriedly been made into an emergency hospital, and the casualties were taken there. There were volunteer stretcher parties that ventured out on the grounds to bring in the wounded or dead, and I wondered then, how anyone could possibly feel safe out in the shanty areas. I was surprised that they had not all been ordered into the building. Several shanties received direct hits, and we saw each casualty being brought in the back entrance and through the passage made between the internees. The sight of some of the injured was too horrible to speak of. During the night, a fire broke out in one of the rooms that had been shelled and again I had to admire the efficiency of the American soldiers—no excitement, no seeming haste, and very little noise—but they certainly got things done. A bucket brigade was formed, and as so many soldiers were busy at their guns and guarding the grounds, the number spared to keep things in order inside was surprisingly few. Many of our men joined in to help, and the buckets were passed one-to-the-other for what seemed an hour until, finally, the fire was under control.

The main kitchen opposite to where we stood was a hive of activity. Workers brewed coffee for the soldiers, workers, and medical staff. There wasn't enough coffee, space, or time to serve all, and poor Eric—I remember how the smell just taunted him and he wished so much for a cup of coffee all night long. It didn't bother me so much because I never was too fond of coffee. Eventually, the sun came up and the Japanese apparently took time out to rest because the firing ceased. Everyone looked very drawn and untidy by this time, so we went to our rooms to try to freshen up a bit, and then the day began. I can't go into details of every day and night as this went on for about a week, and I certainly didn't take any notes during that time or even later about it. Now, it is too difficult to remember exactly what happened and in what order. I only know that the whole week was like a bad dream, and the best I can do is to state the few episodes that are still clear in my mind.

During the first shelling, our very good friend Noble Bradley was stricken with appendicitis and was taken to the education building which had been converted into a hospital. He was operated on, but the poor chap was so undernourished and weak that it was almost too much for him. Then the next day, or perhaps the day after, a direct hit was scored on that building, and although we heard from some that he was hit, we do understand from his wife that it was the shock that ended the life of another friend. He was a man we admired all through the internment; he never grumbled about a thing, and he was always so pleasant and would have some witty, optimistic remark to make whenever the topic of 'how much longer will this go on' came up. He never doubted for a minute that help would come in time, and we were terribly sad at his passing. It would take pages to tell of the other fine people who had clung to life those three years only to have it snuffed out after help had arrived.

During the days, the shelling was usually just spasmodic, and an attempt was made to go about our work as we had to eat and our few clothes had to be washed, etc. What took longer than anything was the waiting in line for water. I never did get it straight as to why the water was disconnected; it seems to me that the supply lines were broken, yet I also remember that the military was afraid the Japanese might poison the water while they still had access to the reservoir. The fact remains that the water was cut off, and it was necessary for us to walk clear to the back gate where the soldiers operated a pump. This never-ending line for water was longer on account of a rule hurriedly issued that said to go to the bathroom, you must bring your own pail of water to flush the toilet. A large drum was placed in each bathroom and filled with water for use during the nights as we were not allowed on the grounds then, but this never was enough, and by morning, especially after heavy gunfire (which made people more nervous and prone to use the bathroom more often), words cannot describe the state things were in. Perhaps I am being a little too outspoken in even mentioning this subject, but then there isn't anything delicate about a war, and when you consider about four thousand people living under such conditions in a building without running water for about two weeks, then you really have a problem. To me, along with the shelling, it was the next major horror. It was an unhappy and unpleasant situation that had to be taken care of, and naturally, by us. When the shelling had ceased altogether, the army did hire Filipino workers to come in daily to clean up, but for a week each bathroom had to be taken care of by the occupants of the room using it. I say here that I did my share, as it was unthinkable that such a burden should fall on a few, but I heard many women say "Oh I just couldn't do it" and it made me feel like barring them the use of the bathrooms. I only hope that I never have to attack such a job again in my life.

One day, Eric was sitting with the children while I stood in line for water, and after what seemed like hours, I was returning with my dishpan as full as I could carry it, when more shells started whistling through the air. They sounded very close and exploded just beyond the grounds, so I hurried to reach the building when another hissed so low overhead that a soldier walking near me dropped to the ground when he heard it coming and yelled to me "Better get down, lady, they're close." But the thing had already passed, so crouching as low as I could (as if that did any good), I hurried on, still with my pan, and I remember feeling so mad at the Japanese, and thinking that I was not standing in line for water to have them frighten me into dropping it. Well, I just reached the building when the next shell hit and people began rushing here and there. I set my pan of water down on the old personal service counter and fled in search of Eric and the children, meeting them coming down the stairs. By then, the lobby was so full of people that the best we could do was to squeeze in with about twenty more in the small square space behind the personal service counter. Almost right away another shell hit the tower and roof and shrapnel and concrete seemed to be flying everywhere. We were not too well protected from anything that might ricochet from the patio walls, and the best we could do for the children was to stand between them and the outside. One of these hits broke the water tank in the roof which had just been filled with the idea of using it for the bathrooms at night. It so happened that this tank was directly above us on the roof, and before long, water started to seep down until we had a complete curtain of water blocking our view and getting us all wet. When this became worse, we all made a dash for one of the downstairs rooms which was full enough before we reached it. More casualties began to come in from the shanty areas and after a while, it seemed that the emergency hospital was full. As shells were hitting the education building, it became no use to take people there, so we were told to vacate that room as they intended to make a hospital out of it. We had to go, but where to stand and be halfway safe was the problem. We just milled about the halls until the shelling ceased, but it certainly was an uncomfortable few hours. Later, I searched for my pan and found it empty, of course, so I had to stand in line again for more water after all.

During these days, one horrible reminder of the tragedy of it all was seen every time we went down the back stairway; there, in full sight, was a room full of sheet-covered bodies with tags on their toes, waiting for the shelling to cease so that they could be buried.

Another day I remember was one when things seemed fairly quiet. Eric was sitting at our table in the hall while I was dressing the children in the room, when all at once a shell hit the roof and a huge piece of shrapnel came clear through the concrete wall just a few feet behind Eric. He fell to the floor very quickly, but it was just the one piece so he got up and we joined him, and all the occupants of the nearby rooms started to make for the back stairs. When we had taken just a few steps down, another hit put a hole through the wall in a direct line with the stairway; where the piece went, I don't know, but cement and dust was falling all over us. Perhaps a piece also went through the downstairs wall or windows—come to think of it, I do remember seeing a hole there later on—however, the people directly below started to come up the stairs and the result was a bottleneck on the landing with neither group wanting to give way. Eventually things stopped falling and we went back to our own floors, but it was silly while it lasted, and we laughed about it later.

Yet another time, when we felt surer of the direction of the firing, a large number of us took our chairs and stools and sat along close to the wall at the back of the building, and in this way at least, we had plenty of fresh air. I remark on this instance just to show how easily people become panic-stricken. We were all sitting outside—talking and so on—when for no apparent reason, all those to the right of us got up one after the other, but so quickly, and started to rush to the doorway.

No one stopped to ask why, yet I had heard no shell explode or gun fired. Naturally, we got up too, and would have been borne inside with the crowd, but an older woman to my left was trying to fold her chair and became entangled in it. The crowd was upon us in a second. If I remember, Eric was a little to the rear and was carried inside with that line of people and didn't notice our dilemma. I pushed the children in front and sort of under me, and had to stand firm because the woman and her chair blocked our way and the crowd was pushing so hard that I couldn't even step to one side of her. People just seemed to pile up and it felt as though there were at least three right on my back. In what seemed like very long minutes, the old lady disentangled herself and we almost fell into the building in a heap. Everyone then stopped and said, "What was the matter?" and so on, but believe it or not, no one knew. There was some vague talk of someone on the end seeing a sniper, but I never did hear if that was so. My poor back ached for days, but had I fallen, I'm sure the children plus myself would have been trampled. Well so much for people's nerves; they were ready to jump at the drop of a hat. Most nights, we found a spot in the downstairs hall where we spread a blanket, and one night the children seemed a bit cold, so I went up to our room to get more covers. It irked me to see their beds and know they might be sleeping comfortably in them and if some of the others had joined me, I would have taken the risk and let the children sleep in peace, but there wasn't a soul in any of the rooms on that floor, and as lights were out everywhere, I had to feel my way. The silence and blackness was really creepy, and when I came out of the room, I don't mind admitting that I fled like one pursued.

After what seemed to us forever, more of Uncle Sam's forces arrived, and then Santo Tomas really energized. Everyone's morale soared when they saw the vast array of tanks, guns, equipment, and men everywhere. Piper Cub planes—or whatever they are called—buzzed low over the city to locate the Japanese guns. As I understand it, and from the noises, our guns were set up a block or two east of the camp, and the infantry started out west to clear the Japanese from the city. What struck me as ironic were the copies of headlines we would read on the noticeboard: "Manila Falls," etc. My goodness, the bloodshed had only just begun, and

I realized it more fully when I came down the front stairs the first day after our men began to spread out from the camp, and there, before my eyes, was the most heartbreaking sight. The whole floor of the lobby was covered with soldiers on stretchers, and they were being sorted out—the dead to one side, and the wounded to the other—to be taken to the clinic for emergency treatment, then to the rooms being used as hospital overflow. It was such a terrible waste of life, and the horror of it all just made me sick. Yet to talk of the futility of war seems a great waste of time. Men have been killing each other since time began, and anything a mere woman might say makes no difference.

By this time, we were back in our rooms at night, but most of the husbands slept in the hall outside to be on hand. We would hear the big guns firing all through the nights—our own louder because they were nearer—then the hiss through the air. By listening carefully, we could hear the explosions way over somewhere in the city. The report from the Japanese gun was not so loud, but the hiss of the shell became louder and louder until the final explosion, which was always near the camp. Sometimes the children would wake and ask, "whose gun was that?" and when I would reply that it was ours, they would go back to sleep quite happily.

Several times the Japanese shells would fall short and start dropping in the grounds again, and then I would bundle up the children, and Eric would come in and carry one while I took the other, and back downstairs we'd go until things had quieted down again. At this date, we had received letters from home, but I'm afraid we were in too dazed a state to even appreciate them fully. In our replies we were not allowed to speak of the shelling, or what was going on as regards the war, and there really seemed little else to speak of because at that time war was about all that filled our thoughts.

With the additional forces came the long-sought good food, and that, at least, gave us something more to talk about. We had been under the impression that the army knew what a weak state we were in and would dole out such food as was suitable (and as much as was good for us), but of course the army had other worries. They had done enough in rescuing us and bringing in the food, and so all the good things were served to us in as large of quantities as we could eat. I'm afraid everyone's eyes were bigger than their stomachs, because they just couldn't stop eating, and of course, their insides were not in a condition to assimilate such rich food and in such quantities, and so large numbers of internees became very ill. Just to cite one item, we were each served a whole large can of evaporated milk every day, and this we poured on our mush straight, enjoying the creamy taste too much to dilute it to milk strength, and you can imagine what this did after not even tasting milk for three years. So much food was served to us that we had a hard time finding enough empty cans to take on the line to collect it. What luxuries they were—canned meats, rich stews with three or four vegetables, all the properly cooked rice we could eat, dehydrated eggs, onions, etc.—we couldn't understand it when soldiers would say how they hated the stuff. But before we were through, we began to understand. There is a richness and sameness about the army food that makes it very monotonous. I remember the first day that bread was brought into camp. There were army trucks full of it, and we stood around with mouths open in wonder while it was unloaded. My, how wonderful food looks to a hungry person.

Luckily, aside from stomach upsets for a few days, we four did not become really sick from overeating, and Eric is to be thanked for it because I'm afraid I would have let the children have all they thought they wanted. He insisted that we take it easy, and so we would save our food and eat small quantities every few hours rather than fewer, larger meals, and I think this did the trick.

As the infantry gained in the city and suburbs, trucks would bring in loads of people rescued from the burning debris. These were people who had miraculously escaped the machine gun fire, grenades, etc. of the Japanese, and had luckily fled in the right direction and found the American lines. Others who fled in what must-have-seemed away from the trouble, were mostly caught up with and killed. The stories of sheer horror that we heard firsthand from some of the rescued people would fill a book and would need to be told by a more capable person than myself. I only want to say here that one person rescued in this manner was our friend Ann Bachrach. If she had stayed in her home in Quezon City, I'm almost sure she would have been unharmed, but when trouble first began, she and her husband went to the city to be near friends. As the Japanese retreated, she and her friends heard of the slaughter so fled, but later, they took shelter in the basement of a house. As the Japanese caught up to that block, they did what they had done with every block before—set fire to each corner house, and as the block went up in flames, machine-gunned the people as they fled to safety. Ann's husband was shot right before her eyes, as were all the people around her, but somehow, she was missed. She fell to the ground anyway and lay amongst the dead and dying for hours, then spent a nightmare four days and nights crawling from one hole to another. She'd had nothing to eat and nothing to drink, and there were fires all around her. In this way, she reached the American lines. When I saw her, I didn't even recognize her, and only after hard scrutiny did I see any familiar sign, and that was just a little indescribable something. She was filthy and spattered with blood. Her clothes were practically in shreds; her face was so thin and ravaged looking, and her eyes were so dark and sunken, that she really looked like a person possessed.

She could not speak coherently, and I doubt if she will ever be her old self again. She was only one of hundreds to go through such an ordeal, and many of the people we heard of but didn't know suffered much more than she did; others, mercifully perhaps, were killed outright.

Not only were whole families blotted out, but whole streets of families, and on and on for blocks and blocks. The most terrible things happened, but I think enough has been written elsewhere for you to have a good idea of all that. It was during these days that our men, who had been searching for Messrs. Grinnell, Duggleby, Johnson, and Larson, found their bodies. They had been shot and buried in shallow graves. What a tragic end for those fine men. Their bodies were returned to camp and after a suitable memorial service, were buried decently.

From the middle of February onwards, groups of people were flown out of Manila to Leyte, then shipped back home to the United States, but we were not among the lucky ones to leave early.

We were all asked where our destination was to be, and naturally, I said Australia. After those years, I couldn't think further than getting home to my mother and Dad and my own people, and at first this was OK'd. We thought, as Eric needed a rest before starting any work, that we could worry about returning to America later, but after a few more days, an announcement was made to the effect that each person must go where the head of the family belonged, and for us, this, of course, meant America. I could have insisted on my rights as an Australian, but it would have meant separating the family and perhaps being dependent on my people for an indefinite period, so we had to accept their ruling and give up the idea of seeing all of you. This upset me greatly and took most of the interest out of things for me.

On March 1, Doris and Gene Mueller came into camp to visit us and it was so nice to see them again. They brought with them our trunk of things that they had saved all those years, and we certainly felt very grateful to them. When they learned that the next day was Eric's birthday, they asked us to get a permit to leave camp for the day, and they would call for us in their car. They had kept their car in the garage all the three years, and luckily, it was never confiscated. Gene also dug up a drum of gasoline that he had buried in a vacant lot, and they were prepared to enjoy themselves as best they could. We spent a lovely day with them and while there, we peeked at our former home. It then housed a Filipino family who seemed to be mostly living on the floors as they had fled from the city with what little they could carry. Doris told us that the owner had sold the house plus all its contents to some German fellow, so there went the last of the things we owned in Manila, unless, of course, they had been looted long before. They drove us back to camp at three that afternoon, and in a few days, we learned of the unhappy end to that day. When they reached their home again, they had a couple of army fellows in for supper and during the evening, Gene looked out and noticed a fire in the garage. He rushed out, but somehow, in trying to put it out, he became enveloped in flames and in his panic, rushed out into the street where the two friends caught up with him, pushed him down and rolled him in the dirt until the flames were out. Then they hailed a passing jeep and took him to the nearest hospital, which at that time, was the old seminary building that we first went to from our home.

The army had taken it over and made a base hospital out of it. Meanwhile, Doris had gone to the garage and luckily managed to put the fire out before it ruined their car. Later, Eric and I took a trip to the hospital to see Gene, and poor fellow was really a mess. He was bandaged from head to toe like an Egyptian mummy and he was still in the hospital when we left Manila. We have heard since that he healed alright, and when they were able, they sold their car and home and have now returned to Switzerland to their people.

A little later in March, Mr. and Mrs. Ipekdjian came into camp and the children, especially, were so happy to see them again. They invited us out to lunch and set the date for within a few days because none of us knew when our names might be listed to be ready to leave Manila. They called for us in their car, and we had a very enjoyable time with them. A nice meal was served outdoors, and while we were there, they told us of the experiences they had. It seems that they stayed in their home, hoping there wouldn't be any danger near them, but sometime during February, a band of Japanese were trying to retake a water reservoir not so far from their home while a group of Americans were guarding it and keeping them off. Unfortunately, their home was in between the two groups, and bullets started to whiz about so they all took shelter in their air raid shelter. This went on for several days and the walls of their house were simply riddled with bullet holes. They had a hectic time making meals of the little food in the shelter, and when that ran out, some of them would crawl to the house to get more. They all became very tired and dirty and were glad when it all stopped. This sounds small trouble in comparison with some, and perhaps I haven't remembered lots of the details. I know that at the time of the telling, it all sounded hectic and dangerous enough to us. Before leaving, we thanked them again for the wonderful care they had taken of the children during the months they were there; I'm sure I will never be able to repay them for their kindness, but I do feel that they believe they have been repaid with their own baby. It was so nice to see how happy they were with the little chap.

As sections of the city were cleared of Japanese, land mines, and the like, we were permitted to walk about the safe areas. One day, I decided to take Ann for a walk as I really thought it would be an education to us to see and remember the place as the Japanese had left it. Perhaps I was thinking in my subconscious mind that the whole city would be cleared and rebuilt in a very short space of time, somewhat like you might clean the dirt from a house, but I understand that now, in May of 1947, things are in just about the same condition as when we left; how depressing that must be to the Filipinos, to have to live year after year in the ruins of their city.

Well, to get back to where I was . . . Eric stayed in camp with John while Ann and I started on this walk. Looking back now, I think it was a very foolish thing to do, and I had no right to leave Ann or myself open to danger the way I did. It so happened, of course, that we were alright, but on thinking of it afterwards, there was a lot that could have happened. Right after leaving the camp, we could see where shells had fallen short of their target and hit private homes and other lesser buildings. Then, as we walked further and finally reached the shopping and business district, we just gasped at the damage that had been done. There wasn't a place left intact, and the Japanese had apparently blown the buildings up then set fire to what was left; at any rate, street after street was just full of empty shells of buildings, with the framework all blackened and charred from the fire.

When we came to the bridge that crosses the river at the top of the Escolta, we found that it was no more—just blown right up. We walked along with others on foot and found they were crossing at a small pedestrian- and light-vehicle bridge that was still in one piece. Once on the other side, we walked back to the Escolta—once the nicest streets in Manila, full of up-to-date stores and fine buildings—but all were gone now, and in most cases, just the shells remained. Some seemed to have escaped fire but had been blown up. Many had fallen right across the street while others were leaning so dangerously that it seemed a gust of wind would knock them down. We passed what was left of the Ipekdjian's jewelry store, and it had fared just as badly as the rest. Except for the Escolta, the streets down as far as the Jones bridge seemed to have been cleared of rubble, etc. and I thought that would be as far as we would be allowed to go. But this bridge had a temporary crossing over it, and traffic was being inspected and allowed to cross. Also, there was a narrow pedestrian path, so I asked one of the MP's on duty if we might go over and he said yes, but not to go too far on the other side. It seemed quite an experience to cross that bridge, as it shook and moved, and generally seemed very insecure. But that just goes to show how deceiving the looks were, because all the heavy trucks passed over that bridge and I understand it is still the main one in use at this date. Once on the other side, things looked different. To the right, ran the road to Intramuros, "The Walled City," and from where we stood, we could see the gaping holes in the ancient-but very-solid walls and the ruined tops of buildings beyond. A notice warned us not to go further in that direction as it was still unsafe. To the left was what was left of the once very-fine post office; shell holes could be seen everywhere, and even the palms nearby had their tops blown off. This area was where an intense battle had raged; the Japanese had holed up in the post office and our men really had to blast them out. The big battle, of course had taken place in the walled city where the Japanese made their last big stand. I understand that they had the population locked in with them, and they had to finally die alongside the Japanese as it was impossible to rescue them, and the place had to be shelled by our men to allow the infantry to get in. We used to hear about those dreadful days firsthand from one of the infantrymen who used to come and talk to us when he had a few hours off. He used to tell us how the Japanese would hide down in the old Spanish wells and our men had to go right up to them and throw grenades down. No doubt the Japanese had it all figured out; theirs was the way to fight a losing battle, but what a lot of precious lives could have been saved had they used a bit of sense and surrendered like a normal enemy. It had all been so recent that as we stood there, I could almost imagine I could see it all. We walked on down the road that leads to the various American clubs and the popular Ermita district, and I hoped to reach these places to see what was left, but it was out of the question as the narrow roadway that had been cleared was just enough for the hundreds of army vehicles rushing back and forth over it. We didn't dare walk on the sides as the rubble was thick, and here and there we saw a hand grenade and large things that looked like unexploded shells; added to that, the smell of the dead not yet collected from underneath the rubble was getting worse as we went along, so we finally turned back. It was such a long walk and although jeeps and trucks and army cars kept passing us, I just couldn't muster the nerve to thumb a ride back to the camp. Most of the way back, I carried Ann on my back, and I was tired when we at last reached Santo Tomas. It had been silly to venture so far as there could easily have been stray snipers left behind. It was possible too, that we might have been accosted by a native, because, after all, it looked odd to see a lone white woman and a small girl walking through those wrecked streets. Eric was cross when we told him how far we had gone, and I didn't blame him.

One other time we were lucky in getting a jeep ride to see the ruins, and we went right out past what had been the Jai-Alai, a once-famous and

very-lovely nightspot that Eric and I often fre-
quented for dinner and dancing. Now, it was lev-
elled so flat that we had to go back over the area
twice to figure out just where it had been. All that
was left was a mass of rubble, and that could be
said of all the Ermita district as well; it was just a
desert of rubble and charred ruins, and it was almost impossible to see where the streets had been.

Filipinos were wandering about the ruins, perhaps looking for something to salvage from the
debris. Where all these homeless people were living, I didn't know, but I think they housed them in
schools and halls, and many were able to double
up with people and relatives whose homes had not
been ruined.

One day late in March, we had a visit from Martin Craven. He had come from the Army hospital
at Muntinlupa. We all expressed relief to find each
other alive and in fair shape, and we exchanged
stories of our rescue. The rescue of the Los Banos
internees was far more spectacular than ours, and
I will tell of it here as Martin told us. Early on the
morning of February 23, the people were up and
about and discussing the plane activities of the
night before, when they saw nine big US transport
planes flying low overhead; they hadn't much time
for thinking when, to their complete surprise,
they saw soldiers parachuting to earth. They were
shooting as they came down, and right away, they
made for the gates and fence of the camp. At the

same time, screaming and yelling Filipino guerrillas rushed from a nearby mountainside, and they
joined in the attack on the Japanese guards and
staff. As if all this shooting, etc. wasn't excitement
enough, they next saw a long column of amphibi-
ous tanks crash their way into the camp. All this,
plus the killing of approximately two hundred Japanese, could be seen by the internees from their
barracks (where they had fled for safety when
things began to pop). They weren't there long however, before the American soldiers ordered them
all to hurry into the amtracks, and this they did,
not waiting to pick up any of their old possessions.
As they roared out of the camp, they could see
the whole place ablaze behind them. They had a
thrilling time crossing Laguna de Bay with bullets whistling past them, but they finally reached
the beach at Cabuyao, and there, they were sur-
rounded by soldiers, war correspondents, guerrillas, and the like. Hot coffee and sandwiches were
served to them, and later, they were all taken to
the army hospital at Muntinlupa to await the
time when they could be sent safely home to the
States. The thing they didn't learn until later was
that the whole elaborate plan of rescue was rushed
through, but with great care, to outsmart the Japanese in charge of the camp, because it had been
learned through guerrillas that February 23 was
the date set for the Japanese to kill everyone in the
camp. It had been planned for roll call time, so if

that had been carried out, the people would have had just a matter of minutes to live when they were rescued so thrillingly right from under the noses of the Japanese.

Martin told us that he and Louise also expected to leave at any time, and it turned out the transport they were on arrived in Los Angeles just a few hours ahead of ours, so we all met again and had time for much talking before they left for Connecticut.

On March 25, at last, we saw our names listed to be ready to leave camp the next morning. I don't have to tell you that we were ready well ahead of time. We were all lined up on the front plaza and took our places in army trucks, and I couldn't help but feel happy at the thought that after seeing so many others leave the same way—but on Japanese army trucks, for Los Banos and other places—that when we left, we left properly, without a Japanese in sight. We took our last look at Santo Tomas, our prison for the past thirty-seven months, and waved goodbye to the people that were left, and off we went.

The column drove through town and through part of the walled city, so we were able to see some of the damage there. We then arrived at the waterfront, and as the wharves and streets had been so badly bombed in this area, it had been necessary for the soldiers to build up a temporary road and wharf. When we finally made our precarious way to the ship's side and went aboard the SS John Lykes, we looked back at the scene of desolation, and it was really pitiful. Our boat was the first to leave the harbor after it had been cleared of mines, etc. and as we picked our way out, wrecks were visible everywhere—ships of all shapes and sizes—and I wondered how many were right on the bottom and out of our sight. I don't think I should dwell on the trip home, because, uncomfortable as it was, it was the accepted mode of travel for the GIs, and if they could take it with a smile, then surely we could.

We were one of a convoy of thirty to forty ships as far as Hollandia, but from there we went on alone. The trip took thirty-six days in all, and until after we left Honolulu, the heat was terrific. One thing I was thankful for was that I wasn't seasick, and this was amazing because I had always been seasick on every sea trip I had taken before. Perhaps my mental attitude had something to do with it, because once aboard, I found that Eric was to be two decks below at one end of the ship while I had to be one deck below at the other end, so he couldn't take the children even if I wanted him to. The reason was that mothers with a child under five years were given the use of the officer's quarters, while men, women, and older children had to sleep in hammocks along with the GIs. Then, too, it was out of the question that the children could be allowed to wander around alone because not only was the ladder to the deck backless and almost perpendicular, but the rungs were just thin steel and quite difficult to manage. Once on deck, care had to be taken that the children didn't go near the sides alone, because they consisted mostly of just two steel chains, so we had to keep constant watch on Ann and John. During the days, we mostly did nothing but sit on a hatch and talk or just sit, but the nights were hard because it was so hot below, more so on account of the heavy curtains used to keep the place blacked out. Until Hollandia, I did not go to bed at all because I had been allowed two bunks, supposedly one for the two children and one for myself, but my kiddies were too long and got their legs tangled, and it was too hot for them to sleep side by side, so I gave them my bunk, and would sit up chatting with other mothers in the same predicament. Toward morning when even black coffee wouldn't keep us awake, I, for one, would just lie front down on one of the wooden benches and take a nap. Often, through the day, I was able to catch another nap when Eric would mind the children. Then at Hollandia, they put on extra folding cots, so I was able to find a spot for mine and at least stretch out at night.

We had "boat drill" almost every day, and there was nerve-racking gun practice which we knew was necessary, but together they reminded us of the threat of Japanese submarines. We thought the climax had come one night toward one o'clock when an urgent order came over the ship's loudspeaker system for all to make haste to their "abandon ship" station. I was fully dressed, as were most of the adults throughout the trip, but I had to rush to dress the children, and while I hurried over that job, I thought it possible that if we ended up in the water I would regret dressing them, but still that might not eventuate, so I had to dress them. People were in a turmoil everywhere, but Ann and John were good and didn't get excited, and I had them up on deck while some were still hunting for clothes. By this time, another announcement came that it was "all clear" and we could relax. What a hectic few minutes they had been, and a couple of women fainted afterwards, perhaps from relief—I wouldn't know. Eric said if the boat had been hit, he wouldn't have had a chance because of all the hundreds of people trying to reach the deck, and he wasn't anywhere near the top when the "all clear" sounded. Later we heard that a submarine had been seen, and it hadn't answered when questioned, so our men had the guns trained on it in a matter of minutes, and I understand would have fired if the submarine hadn't revealed that it was American right at the last second.

We did not land at Honolulu, but stopped quite a way out, though not too far to be able to recognize landmarks. We wished so much that we could land, but permission had not been granted for that, so while we looked and thought of the friends we had there, and of our furniture that had been there in storage for over four years, we had to content ourselves and go on.

How thankful we were when we finally reached Los Angeles the Red Cross said they would send a cable to everyone's next of kin if they so desired—and for nothing. It suited me fine because right then, we couldn't have paid for one, but later, I heard you never even received it, and that was a shame.

Well, Mother and Dad, you know all that has happened since, so I will make this the end.

About December 21 or 22 of 1940, I was a passenger on the Philippine Clipper on a flight to the Philippine Islands from Honolulu. I am almost sure that was the name of the seaplane; in any event, it was a sister ship to the China Clipper.

My husband was already in the Philippines on business, and I was to take the children and join him.

At the time, I was still a British subject lacking only two month's residency on U.S. soil to apply for citizenship. I had already made application for first papers, but since it was necessary to leave United States soil prior to becoming a citizen, I had to obtain what is called a reentry permit.

When I look back at the numerous questions that were asked of me as to why I had to go, etc., it verified my knowledge that relations between Japan and the US were so strained even in 1940, that I marvel that people get so upset about the "sneak attack." It is true that in the so-called *civilized* order of things, there should have been a declaration of war, but since we had them in such a position that nothing short of war would solve it, one cannot be so surprised at their actions. I thought for a while my application might be denied, but it was not. Had I known what was in store for us, I would have stayed in Honolulu and asked my husband to return immediately. However, this is not a story about the war or of our internment in a concentration camp for three years, it is just an anecdote about traveling on the Clipper with two small babies. My daughter, Ann, was twenty-two months old, and John was not quite three months. I remember when I purchased my ticket at the Pan American office and asked about the fare for children, I was told under such and such an age—I forget exactly—it was half price, while under two was free. I said, "well, I have two under two, but would understand if you charged half price for one, though the baby will be in a basket on the floor." I remember how surprised the clerk was when she said "You have two under two?" and I said yes and told their ages. She just smiled and said that was my good fortune, and there should be no charge for them. My husband was hoping to have us in Manila for Christmas, but there was a severe typhoon in the Pacific—that must have been around mid-December, and the flight was delated and delayed. Eventually, it was considered safe enough and I was notified to be ready for an early departure. The first dilemma was that with the limited baggage allowance for one rather than three, meant I had to keep things to a minimum. I bought two large boxes of CHUX disposable diapers for use on the flight, and packed only two dozen of the regular kind. The CHUX were in a separate package for easy access, but in the rush of leaving the house with a small baby in my arms and a toddler in one hand, plus bag etc., my friends carried the other items to the car and then to the airport, and in the general confusion, the package of CHUX were left behind in the house. When it was discovered at the airport, it was too late to do anything, and at that hour, there was no place open to buy more even if they had been available, so I had to start using the two dozen in my bag. I threw the soiled ones out, but had to keep the wet ones to wash out at each stopover. In those days, there was no night flying as there is today and the trip from Honolulu to Manila, or rather Cavite, was four days of flying with a stopover each night at a Pan American hotel. First stop was Midway, then Wake Island, then Guam, and finally Cavite. As I recall, the Clipper was quite small and while it was not filled to capacity by any means, I think there must have been only a dozen passengers in all. I was the only female along with my little Ann. Then, besides the male passengers, there was one steward. They did not have a stewardess. I imagine when the steward saw me boarding with the two small ones, he probably thought "well this is going to be quite a trip," however, they were both very good with John being so young that he slept most of the time. That was a good thing, because on the first day out, Ann and I were airsick all day.

When we arrived at Midway, it was necessary to go from the plane to a little boat and then to the land. I was too busy to find out why, but it must have been some safety measure—perhaps the water was too shallow near the land, or perhaps there was a coral reef or something. Anyway, we were then driven up to the hotel and I remember how concerned the lady was that I had this tiny baby. The China Clipper was in from Hong Kong also with a tiny baby passenger, and they did not have any baby cribs. She said she was certainly going to complain and get that rectified. Actually, it wasn't all that important. I just put John in a regular bed and propped up the side with a pillow under the mattress.

My memory is very hazy as to the room and the dinner, and I certainly could not explore any of Midway since I had my hands full. I had to bathe both children and get them ready for bed, warm John's bottle, feed him and then feed Ann, then get them both to bed. Then I went for dinner. After that, I had to wash out the wet diapers and hang them around to dry.

I was up very early next morning and went to

the kitchen to prepare John's formula and fill several bottles, then had to dress and feed both children and myself before we could be ready to leave. I carried a cloth bag with two wooden handles that I called a *dilly bag*. In it, I kept all the baby's feeding materials: bottles, a jar of sterilized nipples, measuring spoon, funnel, can of formula, etc. However, since my hands were full, I set the bag carefully beside my overnight bag and the other passengers' overnight luggage and someone saw to it that this was all put on board a bus in which we were all driven to the water's edge. From there, we went out on the little boat and boarded the plane. Then everything was closed up for the flight. Unlike in Honolulu, where the required fifteen-minutes warmup period takes place right at the dock, Midway must be in a harbor because while warming up, the plane was able to go slowly out toward the open sea. I was getting the children and myself settled and looked around to check on the dilly bag, but could not see it anywhere, so I asked the steward, and he said he hadn't seen it. Everyone was asked whether they brought it aboard, but no one had seen it, so the steward relayed this news to the Captain, who in turn, must have talked back to the shore, and it turned out that since it was an awkward item, the bus driver had carefully placed it beside his seat while driving, then forgot to pick it up so there it was, still back on the bus. They were instructed to bring it out on the boat and the

Clipper was turned around and headed back. We had been warming up for almost the full fifteen minutes and in just minutes we would have been in the air.

After another fifteen minutes, the plane and the boat came together and the steward opened the emergency exit on the wing, discarded his shoes and socks, rolled up his pants legs and with a boat hook, cautiously went out on the wing. I was feeling like two cents for having caused this trouble, and from where I was sitting, I could see the man in the little boat, standing up and holding out the dilly bag. The steward was holding on with one hand while leaning over and trying to hook the handles of the bag. It seemed as though every time the boat would go down on a wave, the plane would go up, and I wondered if they would ever get together. I also wondered what on earth we would do if the bag fell and went down—how on earth would we feed Johnny. Finally, the steward hooked the handles and proudly brought the bag on board. He then had to button everything up again and get things back to normal, and once more we started out. After we were airborne for a while, the captain handed over the controls and he walked back through the cabin. I thought he was going to bawl me out but he smiled and said "When your boy grows up, you can tell him we turned the Clipper back for him, and this is something we would never do. When we are ready to go, we go. But since there is no way we can feed your baby, it will teach us a lesson to carry emergency supplies of this nature."By the way, years after the war when I thought I might try to write up this little anecdote as a short story, and perhaps earn a few badly needed dollars from a magazine, (which I never did accomplish), I telephoned the Pan American office in San Francisco to verify that they did carry emergency supplies on future flights and was told they did.

While that was probably the high interest point of the flight, I should continue with rest of the trip.

The second stop was Wake Island and the typhoon had been so severe and had done so much damage, that all women folk had been flown off. There was also concern about the purity of the water, and a doctor who was on board even suggested that from then on, I should line the baby's diapers with Kleenex—a precaution which I am sure was unnecessary, even had the water been contaminated. It was very eerie on Wake Island. The wind still moaned, and I had thoughts of the typhoon returning and blowing us all off the place.

After the same busy routine with the children, we took off early the next morning for Guam. This was Christmas Day, and I was not going to make it to Manila in time. As a Christmas gift from Pan American, the passengers were each given a nice little handy clothes brush in a neat leather cover. When you unsnapped the cover and turned it inside out and snapped it again, you could put your hand in it. It was a nice sheepskin polishing cloth. It may sound a strange thing to hold on to, but after one year in Manila, then three in the prison camp, and now back in the States, oddly enough, I have always kept that little gift with me. Christmas afternoon we landed in Guam and were informed that the typhoon had completely demolished the Pan American hotel. The passengers were driven to what seemed like old army barracks. I was assigned to a room and even the door would not close. It had been propped open with a large, heavy chest of drawers. However, I suppose we were lucky to have a place to sleep. I went through the routine of cleaning up the babies and getting them ready for bed, then was driven down to a place like a restaurant. I fed the children, and someone suggested that I take them back to bed then come down myself and have Christmas dinner. That sounded fine, but by the time I got the children settled, I didn't feel right about leaving them, so I told the Guam-native driver that I would not be going back, and if he would like to bring me some coffee and toast, it would do. He took me at my word and brought me back just that. I had thought, perhaps, he might have brought me a plate of dinner even if it wasn't too hot, but no matter, it wasn't important. When we took off on December 26 for the last day of our flight, John's diaper supply was getting very low, and the ones I had washed out were not yet dry, so I draped them over some wires I saw up on the inside of the plane. Later, when the captain came through on this usual good-morning trip, he looked wryly at me, the children, and the diapers, and said "What is this we have here, a Chinese Laundry?" I wouldn't be surprised if today they even carry CHUX disposable diapers if there is a baby passenger.The fourth day of flying came to an end when we reached Cavite, which is some considerable drive from Manila. My husband was there to meet us and to get his first glimpse of John since he had left Honolulu back in the early days of my pregnancy. I think the first thing I said to him was, "Please, get us to a store in a hurry to buy some baby diapers." That was quite a trip, and a lot different to flights today. I have gone twice to Australia from San Francisco, and in fifteen hours' flying time, you are right there. When I look back to the days of the China Clipper, it makes me feel like a pioneer.

At this point I would like to add a few pages to this "Letter to my parents" just to answer some of the questions that have been asked of me. Before being allowed to land, I had to be interviewed by the officer from the immigration department and was told that since I had no valid passport, I would have to be entered to the United States as a visitor, which would mean that within one year, I would have to leave the country. This really upset me as it did not make one bit of sense. I said to the officer that all he would have to do was look at my record and see that I came to America legally under the quota from Australia back in 1938, and that he would also see that I had a re-entry permit to allow me to return. The fact that it was outdated was certainly not my fault, as the war meant that even my British passport was outdated. I reminded him that I had two American children, and how was I going to be tripping off to Canada or anywhere else, then having to worry about getting back to the United States. Here was a good example of how to pass the buck. He informed me that he could do nothing more himself, but that I should write to the Immigration Office (I think the address was in Philadelphia,) and that they would help me. That certainly took the gloss off my arriving in the United States. I complied with his request, but the months went by, and I never did receive an answer from them. However, before the first year was over, the Los Angeles office, being right on the ball, wrote to remind me of the date. They hoped I had made arrangements to leave. This was followed later by another reminder that they hoped it would not be necessary to deport me. At this point, we contacted an attorney (which we could ill afford to do), and told him the story. He said he had never heard of anything so ridiculous and said he would get right on it. He contacted the Congressman for our district and gave him the details. Thanks to him, I then heard from the Philadelphia office telling me to go to the office in Salinas, California and answer any questions they may ask. I did this, and he told me they would be in touch with me. Only then, after a few more weeks, did I get a letter stating that I could stay—as of the status I had in 1938.

Being so grateful after being rescued from the Philippines, it did not occur to us that since the powers that be would not allow us off at Honolulu, it should have been quite in order for us to ask them to send our furniture on to us. Stupidly, we let it all go to a person who paid the three-year storage bill. I do believe the government may have agreed to this since they ship service people's things all over, but we didn't think of it. Now, you ask, where did we go from Los Angeles? As I said before, we didn't have a relative between us. We had no money and no job. My husband telephoned an old school pal of his in Modesto, and this man very kindly told us to come and stay at his place. My relatives in Australia were trying to send us some money to help us, but there was some restriction about sending money out of their country. Later, one amount was allowed, and this really saved the day. Interesting as it may sound, I find that even recollecting these times upsets my nervous system, so I will just say that my husband was lucky in getting a job as Sales Manager to an earth-moving equipment company—a position he held until the beginning of his illness in 1961.

Epilogue

Our ship had stopped in Honolulu to take on fuel. Even though Dad pleaded with the captain to let us disembark, he said no, he was not allowed to do that. Dad had a business partner, friends, lots of help to get us back on our feet, and a storeroom full of our furniture, but the answer was still no. We arrived in Los Angeles June 1, 1945. Many thanks to the Red Cross for the money they gave us to get settled. Dad had several urgent problems on his mind: first was finding housing for his family. Second was finding a job. He managed to get in touch with a few high school friends who had not heard from him in forty years. They were so kind and generous, opening their homes to us. When Dad had finished looking for work in one place without success, we would climb aboard a

Greyhound bus, travel north, and stay again with a friend.

Passing through Gilroy, California on his way to San Francisco by train, Dad noticed a "Hiring" sign for BG Manufacturing Co. He stopped there on his way back, and he had a successful interview. The company was in the middle of constructing new housing for veterans, but it wasn't ready yet. Mr. Graydon Car of the Gilroy Water Department loaned us his summer vacation home in the hills around Gilroy. We stayed there for several months without hot water.

On moving day, the apartment was an excitement we had never experienced. There were three bedrooms, a bathroom, dining room, kitchen, and laundry room, where Mom did all the washing by hand. So much for Dad's promise to her when they were courting that she'd never have to wash another dish. Buying a washing machine was the first big thing I can remember. The next thing was Dad buying a secondhand car.

We made another move to a lovely, bigger apartment several miles out of town when I was a sophomore in high school. My brother and I now rode the bus to school. Mom had taken on a job at a dentist office, so she had to learn how to drive a car.

We had a happy childhood and were active in sports and extracurricular activities.

Both of us attended San Jose State College, but in my junior year, I decided to transfer to the University of California-Berkeley to major in political science. That is where I met my husband-to-be, John Moeller, a Navy officer from Wisconsin. We married in Carmel, California on June 2, 1962. John was finishing his MBA degree at Harvard Graduate Business School, and I found a job doing secretarial work for a large company. John went to work for a large electrical business. The job lasted one year. Then we started to job hunt many times, over and over. If my counting is correct, we moved thirteen times. All told, we had three children—two boys who are one year apart, and a daughter.

My dad was suffering from beriberi, a tropical illness he caught in the Phillpines, and other assorted maladies. He needed to retire, as walking was difficult and tiring. Mr. Albert Gurries (from BG) put Mom and Dad into the job of managing his motel, The Tickle Pink Inn, in Carmel, where they could live in the attached apartment.

Dad died in 1965 in Carmel. Mom continued managing the motel for several years until we needed to bring her to Wisconsin where I could be more help to her. She developed a case of Parkinson's Disease in her seventies, but it was never debilitating. She passed away at age ninety-one in a nursing home in New London, Wisconsin. She wished to be cremated, so we did as she wanted, and interred her ashes in the crematory in West Bend, Wisconsin, where most of our family will find their final home.

My brother, John, married Susan Holbrook, a lovely Californian, in 1965. They had two fine sons who are both wonderful young men. Andrew has two children, and Patrick has three. Susan has retired from teaching and is a very accomplished artist and seamstress.

Unexpectedly, my brother suffered a stroke as a result of carotid artery surgery. We expected him to recover, but it was not to be. John died in the Stanford University Hospital in October, 2017. Five months later, on March 18, 2018 my husband, John, died out of the blue. It took hours for me to realize he had died in his sleep.

I, too, have developed Parkinson's and my children asked me to consider moving to some place closer to any one of them. I was the only person in our family living in Wisconsin. Mark lives in Minnesota, Elizabeth in Texas, and Eric in Virginia. I chose Mark because his home is twenty minutes from my senior living apartment.